SHORT CUTS

INTRODUCTIONS TO FILM STUDIES

FILM AUTHORSHIP

AUTEURS AND OTHER MYTHS

C. PAUL SELLORS

WALLFLOWER

LONDON and NEW YORK

First published in Great Britain in 2010 by
Wallflower Press
97 Sclater St
London E1 6HR
www.wallflowerpress.co.uk

A catalogue record for this book is available from the British Library

ISBN 978-1-906660-24-6

Series design by Rob Bowden Design

Printed in the UK by Cromwell Press Group, Trowbridge, Wiltshire

CONTENTS

ACKNOWLEDGEMENTS

Authorship is a collaborative endeavour. This is not only a thesis of this book but also a fundamental experience of writing it. I would like to thank John Caughie for discussions on authorship in the early stages of this project. Teaching undergraduate and postgraduate students at Edinburgh Napier University has influenced this book substantially by forcing me to re-evaluate my own arguments and presuppositions. When faced with classes of students interested in production, one cannot retreat to the safety of well-trodden academic arguments without sound reasons. Fergus Robb reinforced my interest in film authorship as a collaborative practice by persistently underlining in our conversations the significance of screen-writers in the production process. Roberta McGrath provided invaluable commentary on drafts of the chapters. This book benefitted immeasurably from Giorgio Bertellini's erudite discussions and insightful comments on its every aspect.

INTRODUCTION

Thirty minutes into *Sunset Blvd.* (1950) Norma Desmond (Gloria Swanson), a faded Hollywood star of the silent era who has not worked in the twenty years of sound film, and Joe Gillis (William Holden), a struggling screenwriter, recline on a sofa to watch a film. They are taking a break from working on Norma's script for a new version of *Salomé*, which Joe is revising. The film they watch features, of course, Norma in her prime (really *Queen Kelly* (1929), written and directed by Erich von Stroheim and starring Gloria Swanson). *Salomé* is to be the vehicle for Norma's return to the screen. She plans for the finished script to be submitted to Cecil. B. DeMille (played by Cecil B. DeMille) to direct. In the film DeMille is the director most responsible for Norma Desmond's silent screen stardom, just as he really directed Gloria Swanson at the height of her fame. Max von Meyerling (Erich von Stroheim), her butler, as well as her first husband and the director of her early films, exits the room to start the projection.

Sunset Blvd. (1950): (above left) Joe Gillis (William Holden) and Norma Desmond (Gloria Swanson) watch a silent film starring Norma in her prime; (above right) the film starring Norma Desmond is really *Queen Kelly* (1929), featuring Gloria Swanson

Sunset Blvd. was produced by Charles Brackett, directed by Billy Wilder, and written by Brackett, Wilder and D. M. Marshman Jr. The story reworks themes and plot lines from *Salomé* and *Queen Kelly*, and draws on the biographical details of three of its main actors: Gloria Swanson, Cecil B. DeMille and Erich von Stroheim, not to mention biographies of some of its minor characters and the very history of Hollywood cinema. Who is the author of *Sunset Blvd.*?

The answer 'Billy Wilder' may come to mind because he is the director of the film. Given the significant contributions from others working on the film, and the extent that it incorporates existing material, this answer does not seem entirely justified. Across most of the history of cinema the name of the director has become ingrained in film criticism, film studies and public culture as the author of a film, premised on the belief that he or she retains overall control over its production. Within film studies we still repeat this notion with little reflection. When the question of authorship does surface, it is rarely 'who else may be the author of a film?' or 'how many people contribute to authoring a film?', but 'is there an author at all?' If answered negatively, the name of the director still resurfaces in inverted commas, ideologically and textually separated from the real individual that arrived on set – a fictional surrogate for the flesh-and-blood director. The author, it seems, is a part of film that we simply cannot do without.

Throughout this book I argue that the concept of a film author is indispensable, but that most of our established means for understanding film authorship do not provide robust methodologies for analysing the practical importance of authorship for film production, criticism and history. Studies tend to examine film authors through their traces in film texts. This approach treats authors as symptoms of texts, through repeated motifs and ideological overdeterminations (more on this in chapter one), not their causes. Considering authors as causes of films requires a methodological shift. In order to understand the authorship of any film and the significance of any author, we require a clear definition of the concept 'author', and research that combines empirical investigations into production histories with critical analyses of film texts. A director, or any member of a film's production team, is an author if, and only if, her or his work on the film meets the criteria of the definition. Such an approach to film authorship has begun to take shape in the last two decades.

Historically, two main lines of thought shaped the concept of the film author. First, film industry responses to moral reformists' agendas in the early 1900s, and interest in film from broader modernist art practices, increasingly enabled film to be characterised as both a respectable enter-tainment and an art. This concept of art was quite broad. It included the reproduction of established art, such as plays, prose and poetry, as well as a growing interest in the formal capacities of film, epitomised by the European avant-gardes of the 1920s. Second, film's capacity as a narra-tive medium invited comparison with literature, and with this the literary author. Because film is largely a visual and, for the first thirty years, a silent medium, the film director's work was more visible that the screen-writer's, and as a result frequently attracted public attention.[1] This was aided by growing critical interest in film as art, notably through European (and especially French) ciné-clubs. By the end of the silent period, the combination of these two influences on film production and criticism had firmly established the director as the author and artist of film across the range of film production. Following World War Two, French critics lament-ing the poor state of French film production, and exposed to a wide range of quality American films that had been unavailable throughout the war, reinvigorated debates about the director as the artistic controller of a film. They called for a new cinema that matched the artistic qualities of the best literature, but that was not simply premised on illustrating great stories. Comparisons of the artistic film director, or auteur, with the quality literary author reinvigorated interest in understanding film as a language. In one sense this development was useful, as it focused attention on film as an act of expression, and not simply as a photographically-based medium. However, this comparison also brought with it the full weight of literary theory to account for a wide range of concerns. By conceptualising film through literature, film theorists spoke at length about narrative and visual aesthetics, but resisted considering these within film's collaborative pro-duction framework and reflecting on the impact of collaborative produc-tion on the notion of film authorship.

The problems engendered by this separation of an entrenched auteur-ism from empirical research were made evident to me through a personal embarrassment. In 1995, while a PhD student at New York University, I attended the Edinburgh International Film Festival. I was aware Walter Murch would attend, so I threw a copy of my recently completed essay on

THX 1138 (1971) into my luggage. I was quite interested in a tiny sound edit in the *Buck Rogers* trailer that opens the film. The phrase '25th Century' had been changed to '20th Century', which placed the film's diegesis in the immediate, not distant future. I was able to speak to Murch in the bar after his talk and I asked him about this edit. He indicated I was correct and the first person to mention this to him in the 25 years that the film had been in circulation. He even pointed out, if I recall our discussion accurately, that Warner Bros. had mis-advertised the film as a twenty-fifth-century fiction. Thrilled at my own attentive reading of the film, I handed a copy of my essay to Murch and left. I was horrified when I later re-read the essay. I mentioned Murch's production roles, including his sound editing, but with the most appalling auteurism credited the film relentlessly to George Lucas. I know why I did this, and why auteurism is so thoroughly embedded in film theory and criticism. Nevertheless, I knew at that moment I had been conceptually sloppy and had denied Murch credit for his intellectual contribution to the film. I doubt this bothered Murch much, but it bothered me. My auteurist presumptions had allowed me to become too enamoured of my own critical capacities, at the expense of considering properly who contributed to producing, in what way, and for what purpose, this entertaining and intellectually engaging film.

In this book I evaluate a wide range of canonical arguments about film authorship to identify the methodological foundations and critical biases that underscore them. In chapters one and two I scrutinise the more conventional theories of film authorship and the literary arguments on which they are based, ranging from the Romantic notion of the author to the poststructuralist dismissal of authorial intention. Next, in chapter three, I discuss the relationships between authors and narrators to explain and illustrate the differences between telling a story and conveying a meaning through film. Drawing this distinction allows me to resolve the central problem of interpretation that motivates arguments challenging authorial intention. In the fourth chapter I examine a number of films as case studies to challenge the Romantic notion of film authors and demonstrate how socially and culturally connected films and their authors are. The very notion of cinematic expression relies upon shared knowledge and conventions between the filmmaker and the film's spectators. Lastly, in chapter five, I discuss contemporary developments in theories of film authorship. These are informed mainly by recent debates in film historiography and analytical film theory, and are characterised by the belief that the study of authorship is an empirical question of a film's construction. These arguments typically endorse authorial intention and collaborative authorship, although perspectives on these concerns vary.

Before delving into chapter one, there are three further points I would like to signal to the reader. First, I have avoided the convention of supplying the director's name in brackets after the title of a film. A central tenet of my argument is directors are not necessarily the authors of films, and when they are they will rarely be the sole authors of films. To add these names would contradict in practice a point I argue rigorously throughout the book.

Second, one of the main problems facing theories of authorship in any medium is critics will locate meanings not intended by the authors. These are often referred to as 'textual meanings' and have been used to justify anti-intentionalist arguments maintaining that authors have no authority over the meaning of a work when it is in circulation. I challenge this model throughout the book and defend an intentionalist view of authorship to combat it. To overcome the problem of unintended meaning I rely extensively on E. D. Hirsch Jr's distinction between meaning and significance (see 1967: 8, 139–44). Meaning refers to authorial intention, significance to other understandings and judgements that spectators bring to the process of reading. This model has a benefit over the anti-intentionalist's argument. Both meaning and significance accommodate plurality at the point of reception, but only by retaining a notion of authorial meaning can a theory of authorship explain authors' ownership and accountability for their expressions.

Third, I will steer clear as much as possible from discussing film authors as artists or auteurs, referring to this concept only as required by my research. Discussions of auteurs and auteurism are generally located in chapter one. This is a book about film authorship in general, and therefore the arguments must apply equally to acts of authorship that produce the most engaging and the most turgid films. I am not arguing against the notion of the auteur in principle, only against the assignment of the director as auteur as a critical accolade rooted in the critic's personal preferences. I define an auteur as an author who produces art through her or his acts of authorship. As I do not forward a theory of art here, I refrain from acclaiming any filmmaker an auteur.

1   FILM DIRECTORS AND AUTEURS

At first glance the notion of authorship in film seems straightforward. Books on Hitchcock, Fellini, Welles, Bergman, Spielberg, Lynch, Kubrick and Griffith, or phrases such as 'Frank Capra's *It's a Wonderful Life*', or '*Crouching Tiger, Hidden Dragon*, a film by Ang Lee', suggest a strong propensity to consider a film's director as its author. There are exceptions where actors, screenwriters or producers are recognised as the central contributor to a film, such as *Rocky* (1976) written by and starring Sylvester Stallone, and directed by the relatively unknown John G. Avildsen, but these are not as common. Some of these directors have even been given the status of auteurs, which elevates them to 'film artists', based on critical assessments of their cinematic outputs. Alfred Hitchcock, Federico Fellini, Orson Welles and Ingmar Bergman have all, by consensus, been elevated to this pinnacle of directorial acclaim because of the stamp of individuality each weaves into the fabric of his films. Other directors, like Michael Curtiz and Stanley Donen are often considered *metteurs-en-scène*. *Metteurs-en-scène* are frequently, though not always, highly competent directors, but their personalities generally are not evident in the films they direct.[1] The classification of some directors proved to be controversial. Critics writing for the French journal *Cahiers du cinéma*, and those writing for the British journal *Movie*, contested Vincent Minnelli's status as either auteur or a highly talented *metteur-en-scène*. This attempt to single out distinguished directors has been historically important for the study of film. If film is to be seen as an art form, and more than just entertainment, it is essential to be able to locate film artists.

This relationship between the film director and film, cast as a relationship between an artist and a work of art, is not as straightforward as the relationship between, for instance, a painter and a painting or a writer and a work of literature. Despite the predominant view of the director as the controller of a film's aesthetic and semantic dimensions, other modes of production nevertheless exist. For instance, the highly-acclaimed National Film Board of Canada Unit B documentary films of the 1950s and 1960s were unit productions, with director, producer, cinematographer and editor credits being attributed to members of the unit as a result of the perceived balance of input during the production, rather than any clearly defined roles (see Harcourt 1977). More fundamentally, the role of the director is historically variable. Janet Staiger points out in 'The Hollywood Mode of Production to 1930' in *The Classical Hollywood Cinema: Film Style and Mode of Production to 1960*, a book co-authored with David Bordwell and Kristin Thompson, that the organisation of film production roles has altered from the beginning of the medium, and that meaning and aesthetic practice are in many ways dependent upon the particular mode under which a film was produced (see Bordwell *et al.* 1985: 85–153). We must also remember that film is most frequently produced collaboratively. Any theory of authorship must accommodate, or at least account for, these facts of production.

Films, initially, were not marketed by the name of the director, or even by film titles, but by proprietary technology: 'It was the Cinematograph, the Biograph, or the Vitascope that were advertised on the variety bills in which they premiered, not *The Baby's Breakfast* or *The Black Diamond Express*' (Gunning 1991: 42). Within a few years this practice gave way to the culture of corporate branding, casting films as manufactured products to be distributed and sold. Eileen Bowser notes that 'exhibitors, exchanges and the public were expected to request films by company names, not specific titles or stars' (1990: 103). Those that directed films (and we must be careful how we use that term for early cinema) were doing so as employees of companies, with the principal responsibility for producing saleable goods. It was largely the market opportunities in vaudeville, music halls and fairgrounds that helped to direct the film industry towards entertainment. Perhaps ironically, our historiographical interest in the development

The Dream of a Rarebit Fiend (1906): complex superimpositions and camera movements convey the character's drunkenness

The 'Teddy' Bears (1907): an early example of stop-motion animation

of narrative film, film as expression, film as art and so on, has wrenched a number of directors, especially pre-1908, out of industrial obscurity. Crediting Edwin S. Porter with the inventiveness of a multiple exposure shot to convey drunkenness in *The Dream of a Rarebit Fiend* (1906) – a shot that anticipates the type of character psychology practised by the French Impressionist filmmakers of the 1920s – or the animated bears in *The 'Teddy' Bears* (1907), accurately indicates a production role but relies upon a concept of a film director that was foreign to the industry at the time.

In his book *D. W. Griffith and the Origins of American Narrative Film: The Early Years at Biograph*, Tom Gunning reminds us that authorship is not a concept that we can assign as easily as our critical practices today suggest. Griffith worked for American Mutoscope and Biograph from 1908 as director and later supervising director of the company's output. The notion of the director that we understand today differs from the concept of the director circulating in the early years of film. Referring to arguments by Charles Musser and Janet Staiger, Gunning notes that initially films were controlled by the camera operator or were produced collaboratively between the camera operator and, following theatrical conventions, the person in charge of rehearsing the actors. 'The concept of the director as a unifying force was not a factor' (1991: 46). During Griffith's time at Biograph, however, he, along with other 'directors', altered this approach, by both directing the actors and determining the formal techniques of their films to enhance their dramatic qualities. His efforts went largely unacknowledged, so on 3 December 1913, he took out a full-page advert in the *New York Dramatic Mirror*, itemising a few of his 'innovations', such as the 'large or close-up figures, distant views as represented first in Ramona, the "switchback", sustained suspense, the "fade out", and restraint in expression, raising motion picture acting to the highest plane which has won for it recognition as a genuine art'.[2] Through this ad he rescued his contributions from the anonymity of corporate employment. At the time that scientific labour management was gaining strength across industries, Griffith established that the films he was involved with were artisanal. Griffith was by no means the 'innovator' of the formal techniques that he lays claim to. Many of these he adapted from nineteenth-century literature or adopted from other films. A mere glimpse of Pathé's *The Physician of the Castle* (1908) and Biograph's (or Griffith's) *The Lonely Villa* (1909) indicates just how much Griffith was prepared to borrow. Rather, what he did, as Gunning identifies, was consider the integration and presentation of the film as a whole. 'The dramatic purpose within a scene

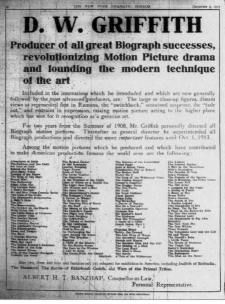

Griffith asserts his role as film artist over Biograph employee in the *New York Dramatic Mirror*, 3 December 1913

determined its visual presentation as well, creating a filmic discourse which expressed dramatic situations' (1991: 47). From our critical and theoretical standpoint it is tempting to cast Griffith as *the* author of the Biograph films he directed, since he maintained primary control over the productions. But as we have seen, this requires different conceptions of both authorship and film than were considered in the early years of Griffith's career (between 1909 and 1913), and also subordinates all contributions within a film to Griffith's control over the project. Gunning argues that the narrator system that Griffith was so instrumental in developing implies authorship. To some degree this is true, but the films are more than mere narratives, which leaves space for contributions by other members of the production to contribute to the meaning, aesthetics and emotional tenor that these films communicate. Billy Bitzer's cinematography and the performances of actresses like Lillian Gish and Mae Marsh, for a start, are too significant for the value of Biograph films, and later Griffith's own projects, to elide or simply to attribute to Griffith's direction. The variable levels of restraint of acting across many of Griffith's films suggest his control over performances was not total. When Griffith left Biograph his ensemble and crew went with him. It is not unreasonable to think that the success of the post-1913 films that Griffith directed owed a great deal to the particular group of people he collaborated with. Griffith certainly is *an* author of the films he directed, but not solely.

Such auteuristic views have become pervasive in film studies, and combined with rigorous, often archival research can, without proper methodological care, distort production histories and our very understanding of the films under investigation. Charles Musser, in his remarkable book *Before the Nickelodeon: Edwin S. Porter and the Edison Manufacturing Company*, challenges the view that the art of narrative film begins with Griffith, and makes no secret that he intends to write a biographical history of Porter's contribution to film before Griffith. His auteurist intentions seem clear when he contextualises his project with auteurist directors. 'Although many books have been written on D. W. Griffith, John Ford, and Orson Welles, not one has been published on the creator of *The Great Train Robbery*' (1991: 1). In the sense that Musser singles out Porter from within the Edison Manufacturing Company, this book is a work on authorship, but it differs from conventional auteur criticism in two important and related ways. First, Musser does not resort to evaluative claims like 'artist' or 'genius', instead analysing Porter's cinematic output in the context of the Edison Manufacturing Company. For Musser, the notion of an artist or genius 'became a methodological category that obfuscated the need for more critical insights' (1991: 2). Second, the primary research materials are not critical analyses of the films, but archival records. Musser explains Porter's contribution to cinema primarily within industrial rather than artistic terms, noting further that employees at Edison, including Porter, worked collaboratively. Analysing Porter's output strictly in artistic terms would have been quite an act of revisionism, given that Porter and the Edison Manufacturing Company were basically producing films to sell by the foot. To ignore Porter's aesthetic contributions would be equally limiting. Many films produced by Porter and his colleagues demonstrate substantial degrees of creativity and aesthetic flair. The objectives of Musser's historical project must be kept clear, though. He is not recovering a long-lost artist of the cinema, since spectators at the time did not generally consider film an art and were unaware of the individuals that made the films. Instead, Musser's detailed analysis of Porter's role in film history and Porter's position within the Edison Manufacturing Company is dependent upon and speaks to our contemporary understanding of film and our privileging of directors as the authors of their films.

Coney Island at Night (1905): Porter uses the lights to mask the architecture

The idea that a cultural artefact can be attributed to the ingenuity of an individual is an old idea, much older than film. Auteurism in film is rooted in the Romantic concept of the author. Andrew Bennett characterises the Romantic author as:

> both an exemplary human and somehow above or beyond the human, as literally and figuratively *outstanding*. He is, after all, ahead of his time, avant-garde. The idea of the Romantic author is opposed to the idea of the writer, the scribbler, the journalist or literary drudge and is conceived as a subject inspired by forces outside himself, forces that allow him to produce work of originality and genius. (2005: 60; emphasis in original)

In his 1948 essay 'The Birth of a New Avant-Garde: La Caméra-stylo', Alexandre Astruc argues that for film to be realised fully as an art it must be capable of individual expression. In order to achieve this, film must become a language, 'a form in which and by which an artist can express his thoughts, however abstract they may be, or translate his obsessions exactly as he does in the contemporary essay or novel' (1968: 17–18). His metaphor of the 'caméra-stylo' (camera-pen) is intended to shift films from being illustrative to being 'equivalent, in their profundity and meaning, to the novels of Faulkner and Malraux, to the essays of Sartre and Camus' (1968: 20). He singles out filmmakers such as Welles, Jean Renoir and Robert Bresson as the vanguard in this avant-garde.

Astruc's call for an avant-garde was not new, and in many ways echoed manifestos about art and cinema from the silent period. He was well aware of this and distanced himself from such an interpretation of his writing:

We have no desire to rehash those poetic documentaries and surrealist films of twenty-five years ago every time we manage to escape the demands of a commercial industry. Let's face it: between the pure cinema of the 1920s and filmed theatre, there is plenty of room for a different and individual kind of filmmaking. (1968: 21)

Although he was proposing a new cinema, his concept of the film author is too reminiscent of debates in the early 1920s to ignore. Richard Abel points out that the notion of film language was 'commonly assumed by most French writers, from Vuillermoz to Moussinac or Epstein' (1988b: 206). Ricciotto Canudo elaborates quite substantially on the notion of cinematographic language in his 1923 essay 'Reflections on the Seventh Art'. In 1924 Jean Epstein advocated a 'new avant-garde', arguing that film should be symbolic, and not a means of reproducing other works of art (see Epstein 1978). Key critics also 'tended to focus on the unity and coherence of the work as a whole, the controlling vision of the filmmaker as *auteur*' (Abel 1988b: 213; emphasis in original).[3] Astruc's statement 'the scriptwriter directs his own scripts; or rather, that the scriptwriter ceases to exist, for in this kind of filmmaking the distinction between author and director loses all meaning' (1968: 22) is prefigured by Louis Delluc in 1923: 'In truth, someone who writes a drama for the cinema must direct it himself' because 'having thought through and experienced a visual composition is the best assurance that they will know how to execute it' (1988b: 285–6). Astruc, in 1948, and Léon Moussinac, in 1921, both single out and criticise Jacques Feyder for the same reason: for illustrating a narrative rather than approaching it cinematically (see Astruc 1968: 19; Moussinac 1988: 252). Lastly, the films that interested these 1920s critics and filmmakers could hardly be reduced to poetic documentaries, surrealist films, pure cinema and filmed theatre, as Astruc suggests, focusing also on narrative films from around the world, notably American and Swedish films.

I raise this not to suggest that Astruc seems well-read, but to demonstrate instead that the Romantic notion of authorship, and the idea that the director, or writer/director, is the author of a film, is deep-seated. French theory and criticism in the silent period was reasonably sophisticated and clearly articulates the notion of the single author as a property of artistic media. Whether it was the screenwriter or director that should be given the authorial accolade was determined by analysing precisely what type of art film was. These ideas then fed back into filmmaking. Two central themes circulate in the critical writings of the 1920s. First, as Elie Faure states, 'the cinema has nothing in common with the theatre save this, which is only a matter of appearances, and the most external and banal experiences at that: ... a collective spectacle having as its intermediary an actor' (1988: 259). Second, of all arts film is closest to music. Germaine Dulac explains the reason behind this:

> Should not cinema, which as an art of vision, as music is an art of hearing, on the contrary lead us toward the visual idea composed of movement and life, toward the conception of an art of the eye, made of a perceptual inspiration evolving in its continuity and reaching, just as music does, our thought and feeling? (1978b: 41)

Authorship, rather than French film theory and practice of the 1920s, is our main interest, but to help to understand the relationship between an author of film, the films that he or she produces, and the history of film authorship that auteur criticism relies on, it will be useful to sketch out some of the core ideas about filmmaking that circulated in French ciné-clubs and journals.

The music analogy developed beyond a relationship with isolated senses. Dulac further explains that music is composed purely of sound, cinema of light. Both are time-based media that require consideration of rhythm and pacing. Most importantly, she proposes that music is an artform that affects the listeners' emotions. By advocating a cinema distanced from theatre, Dulac does not restrict filmmaking to abstract, non-narrative films, such as those by Man Ray, Hans Richter or Fernand Léger. The filmmaker is not prohibited from narrative or even adaptation, but from subordinating the film to the objectives of the antecedent source. 'The cinema can certainly tell a story, but you have to remember that the story is nothing. The story is surface' (1978a: 34). The problem with cinema, she argues, is that its practitioners have been concerned with the wrong issue. Rather than story, the filmmaker, like the composer and

'Desert-like snow' in *The Outlaw and His Wife* (1918)

musician, should appeal first and foremost to spectators' emotions through cinematic, rather than dramatic means.

To do this, filmmakers must consider the nature of the images that they create. Louis Delluc proposed the notion of *photogénie*. Richard Abel describes *photogénie* as recording reality, but transforming it into something else. Through cinematic, rather than photographic properties, 'especially framing, lighting and mise-en-scène relations within the frame', as well as motion and the passage of time, the image revealed something, such as the despair represented in the 'desert-like snow' in Victor Sjöström's *The Outlaw and His Wife* (1918) (1988a: 109–10). Jean Epstein took the notion of *photogénie* to heart. It was not something reproducible, but inextricably linked to the artistic essence of the filmmaker:

> Mechanically speaking, the lens alone can sometimes succeed in revealing the inner nature of things in this way. This is how, by chance in the first instance, the *photogénie* of character was discovered. But the proper sensibility, by which I mean a personal one, can direct the lens towards increasingly valuable discoveries. This is the role of an author of film, commonly called a film director. Of course a landscape filmed by one of the forty or four hundred directors devoid of personality whom God sent to plague the cinema as He once sent the locusts into Egypt looks exactly like this same landscape filmed by any other of these locust filmmakers. But this landscape or this fragment of drama staged by someone like Gance will look nothing like what would be seen through the eyes and heart of a Griffith or a L'Herbier. And so the personality, the soul, the poetry of certain men invaded the cinema. (1981: 23)

Epstein's interest in the aesthetic and formal qualities of the image and film construction, along with other French cineastes, was aimed at developing a modern film art. This did not presume a rigid break with Romanticism. Romantic melodramas, as Dulac suggests, could comfortably coexist with modern film aesthetics and form, if considered appropriately. More significantly, these critics and filmmakers perpetuated in film, with little interrogation, the very relationship that the Romantics had established between an artist and a work of art.

The similarities between the French critics and filmmakers of the 1920s and those of the 1950s and 1960s do not end there. In the journal *Le Film*, Louis Delluc not only wrote favourably about some of the early Impressionist films in France, but also, in 1919, called for the inauguration of a ciné-club that would support international and experimental filmmaking. This model eventually developed across Europe in the mid-1920s and was crucial for supporting the Film Europe agenda, a joint European effort to produce, distribute and exhibit European films, including European 'art' films, in order to help stem the tide of American films that infiltrated Europe following World War One. Ciné-clubs and art theatres, film publications and the connections European film had with other modernist arts influenced policies to collect and preserve many of the art films that were produced and circulated within this exhibition network. The 1930s saw institutions formed such as the National Film Archive in London, the Museum of Modern Art in New York and the Cinémathèque Française in Paris. Michel Marie is correct, therefore, when he notes that Jean-Luc Godard was wide of the mark when he stated that he and his colleagues in the French New Wave were the first generation of directors with extensive knowledge of

Film director as author: Gance's *La Roue* (1923)

Epstein's *La Glace à trios faces* (1927)

Kirsanoff's *Ménilmontant* (1926)

film history (2003: 44). What Marie does not mention is that the consequences of this first French avant-garde enabled the second. Its emphasis on the director as artist, the alignment of small-scale filmmaking with the broader arts, its culture of film criticism, and its archival movement developed the very conditions that enabled the French New Wave.

As we have seen, both avant-gardes relied upon the notion of film language as a vehicle for personal artistic expression. The argument states that if we have a film language, then we have film authors, and vice versa. Those that can compose in film language are capable of individual expression and are therefore film artists, while those that illustrate antecedent texts through the camera are not. The argument does not work, though. To begin with, there is no clear way to determine when a shot, sequence or film reaches the threshold of 'being cinematic', unlike the threshold of sense with natural language. Further, language is not a means of distinguishing artists, but of communicating. A novel by Jackie Collins and a novel by James Joyce are both written in language. Both are authored, and it is the job of the critics and readers of the works to establish their relative aesthetic and semantic values.[4] By crediting the director with visual aesthetics and 'film language', the argument presumes a theory of expression that will inherently bias critical approaches towards the director, since contributions from other members of the production team are generally discounted as only serving the needs of the director. This argument lacks empirical grounding. Throughout this book I will provide further reasons to question the *automatic* assignment of authorship to a film's director.[5]

François Truffaut and others at *Cahiers du cinéma* retained the Romantic notion of the artist and privileged the director in film production, and for the same basic reasons as Astruc. But Truffaut, in his seminal and polemical essay 'A Certain Tendency of the French Cinema' (1954), and in his arguments about the '*politique des auteurs*', or author's policy, does nothing less than reconceive the project of film criticism as a step in reinvigorating film production in postwar France. No longer is the film the main object of the critic's attention, but the auteur that *conceived* and *created* the film. Truffaut distinguishes commercial craftsmanship in what he calls, pejoratively, the 'tradition of quality', found in French film production, from cinematic artistry. He establishes his position on two principles. First, there is a difference between a director who creates a work of cinema and one who films a scenario. Describing the products of the latter as 'scenarists' films', and their directors as *metteurs-en-scène*, Truffaut complained that when scenarists 'hand in their scenario, the film is done; the *metteur-en-scène*, in their eyes, is the gentleman who adds the pictures to it and it's true, alas!' (1976: 233). Second, postwar French cinema, constituting over one hundred productions a year, was dominated by what he calls 'psychological realism'. He finds the narrative scope of these films remarkably limited:

> It's always a question of a victim, generally a cuckold. (The cuckold would be the only sympathetic character in the film if he weren't always infinitely grotesque: Blier-Vilbert, etc ...). The knavery of his kin and the hatred among the members of his family lead the 'hero' to his doom; the injustice of life, and for local colour, the wickedness of the world (the cures, the concierges, the neighbours, the passers-by, the rich, the poor, the soldiers, etc ...). (1976: 232)

Truffaut describes such films as nothing more than formulaic commercial enterprises with the surface appearance of a sophisticated pedigree rooted in the works of Franz Kafka and Gustave Flaubert. He concludes that this literary pretence produces films that are not cinematic, just bad. His objection to such films is more pragmatic than principled. The sheer mass of such films not only squeezes out better ones, he insists, but also deteriorates 'public comprehension when faced with such new works as *Le Carrosse D'Or* (*The Golden Coach*), *Casque D'Or*, not to mention *Les Dames Du Bois De Boulogne* and *Orphée*' (1976: 234). The difference between good and bad films is not in the narratives, but in the audiovisual registers:

> Long live audacity, to be sure, still it must be revealed as it is. In terms of this year, 1953, if I had to draw up a balance-sheet of the French cinema's audacities, there would be no place in it for either the vomiting in *Les Orgueilleux* (*The Proud and the Beautiful*) or Claude Laydu's refusal to be sprinkled with holy water in *Le Bon Dieu Sans Confession* or the homosexual relationships of the characters in *Le Salaire De La Peur* (*The Wages of Fear*), but rather the gait of *Hulot*, the maid's soliloquies in *La Rue De L'Estrapade*, the *mise-en-scène* of *La Carrosse D'Or*, the direction of the actors in

> *Madame de* (*The Earrings Of Madame De*), and also Abel Gance's
> studies in Polyvision. You will have understood that these audaci-
> ties are those of *men of the cinema* and no longer of scenarists,
> directors and litterateurs. (Ibid.; emphasis in original)

Underscoring Truffaut's position, as with the first French avant-garde, is a
form of medium specificity – a belief that there are some defining or unique
qualities of a medium that should be exploited. An artist, on such a view,
is someone that first and foremost understands and exploits her or his
medium. Only by exploring the medium will a filmmaker be able to exploit
a story. It is not enough to achieve this once. Proficiency in a language,
linguistic or cinematic, cannot be judged through a single instance. For
Truffaut and the other *Cahiers du cinéma* critics, one film is not sufficient to
judge whether a director is worthy of the badge of auteur. Any director can
make, on occasion, a film that is enjoyable, but only cinematic artists will
have the knowledge and skills to consistently communicate stories cinematically. This argument produces a degree of circularity. Once identified,
this mark of a personal, cinematic style elevates the director to an artist
of the cinema. The filmic production of such an artist will subsequently
be deemed to be art, mainly because art is being defined as a form of
personal expression from an artist. Edward Buscombe sums up the manifestations of this nicely: 'The belief that all directors must be either *auteurs*
or *metteurs-en-scène* led inevitably to a kind of apartheid, according to
which, as Rivette says, the failures of the *auteurs* will be more interesting
than the successes of the rest' (1981: 25).

The *Cahiers du cinéma* critics were interested in reinvigorating not
only French film production, but also the broader cultural aspects of
the medium. Here history has favoured American film production. Peter
Wollen reminds us that during World War Two the Vichy government and
the German Occupation banned American films. After the war American
films flooded into France and were screened in the ciné-clubs and at the
Cinémathèque Français in Paris. This enabled concentrated, close scrutiny
of the cinematic output of individual directors in a way generally not experienced under normal distribution patterns. Resultantly, French film critics
recognised stylistic and thematic continuities in American films through
the intellectual and critical framework well established in the French ciné-
clubs and film journals (see Wollen 1972: 74–7). Andrew Sarris adds that

the French critics did not focus on dialogue to the extent that the American critics did, and attributes to French critics at *Positif* and *Cahiers du cinéma* a sharper visual acumen with American films than that possessed by American critics (1996: 29).

The *Cahiers du cinéma* approach to auteur criticism does not constitute a theory. At its core there is no rigorous analysis of language, film language, authors, artists, art or cinematic art to justify this critical approach. It relies on the notion that some films are 'cinematic' while others are not. Although treated as a property of a film, the term 'cinematic' is really a term of critical appreciation. *Precisely* what is meant by 'cinematic' is not entirely clear, as the critical discrepancies between *Cahiers du cinéma*, *Positif* and the British journal *Movie* suggest. Then again, criticism is not, nor should it be, a science. Across these journals an agenda developed advocating improved film literacy for the audience, critic and producer of film: a literacy favouring personal expression over commercial interests. This did not result in a purely polemical relationship between expression and industry. Indeed, the majority of directors critically deemed to be auteurs by film journals worked in commercial cinema. The deciding factor focused on whether a director could distinguish her, or most likely his films from the general culture of commercial film production. Her or his films needed to betray the presence of a thinking individual structuring and controlling the film. A Hollywood director could become an auteur not because of the industry, they argued, but despite it. This approach to film criticism has become somewhat naturalised. It is important therefore to indicate some of its main methodological shortcomings. First, it avoids serious consideration of collaborative contributions in film production.[6] Second, it constitutes, as the name suggests, director criticism rather than film criticism. Third, the focus on singling out authorial properties from a collected body of films by a single director may say more about the critic's proclivities than the director's abilities. Fourth, it risks separating individual films from their contemporary film cultures by rooting the analysis of films in the director's mind rather than in the time and place of their construction.

Despite these limitations, Andrew Sarris bolstered auteur criticism by attempting to turn it into a theory of film history.[7] The history of American cinema, he argues, has been blighted by two main concerns.[8] First, America's industrial model of cinema distracted historians and critics from seeking instances of individual, usually directorial, achievement in American filmmaking because films were seen to be subordinate to such things as front-office intervention and industry censorship. Critics subsequently concentrated on non-industrial models of filmmaking as the locus of art cinema and celebrated a range of filmmakers from around the world ahead of American directors.[9] Second, film critics have been too keen to view films as works of sociology rather than works of art.[10] He complains that this resistance to consider American films and their directors seriously and systematically risks historical ignorance of such an important contributor to cultural life. Sarris's theory of history lacks methodological rigour, though, as Sarris himself recognised in the late 1970s (see 1996: 278). His earlier argument turned out to be more a *proposal* for a history than a theory of one. He hinges his 'historiography' on categorising both films and directors as 'good' and 'bad' but offers rather limited criteria for assessing quality outside of personal preference, and the capacity for a collection of films to display 'the distinguishable personality of the director' (1985: 537).[11] These critical assessments are not absolutes, but 'relative standards' based on an accumulative understanding of films produced (Sarris 1996: 35).

Although Sarris did not elaborate on his criteria for film evaluation, he also did not advocate *simply* deferring to the 'whims' of the critic:

> With a 'you-see-it-or-you-don't' attitude toward the reader, the particularly lazy auteur critic can save himself the drudgery of communication and explanation. Indeed, at their worst, auteur critiques are less meaningful than the straightforward plot reviews that pass for criticism in America. (1996: 32)

Although the criteria for assessment are opaque, the process is not. Auteur criticism for Sarris is a comparative process premised on an extensive understanding of a range of directors and their films in order to assess relative levels of quality. In his discussion of King Vidor, for instance, Sarris compares two similar scenes between *The Big Parade* (1925), directed by Vidor, and *All Quiet on the Western Front* (1930), directed by Lewis Milestone, to evaluate the directors' qualities relative to each other. In both films the protagonist (played by John Gilbert in *The Big Parade* and Lew Ayres in *All Quiet on the Western Front*) ends up in a bomb crater with an enemy soldier he has mortally wounded (a German and Frenchman respectively). Unwilling to kill the enemy soldier face to face, the protagonist in each film offers some compassion while struggling with his conscience as the enemy slowly dies. Sarris prefers the scene from *The Big Parade* because Vidor places the camera closer to the actors, producing greater 'dramatic intensity' than Milestone's 'pictorial' image achieves.

Jim (John Gilbert) struggles with his conscience in *The Big Parade* (1925) ...

Sarris does not explain *how* this allows him to conclude that the difference between Vidor and Milestone is the difference between 'an auteur versus a technician. The auteur theory can only record the evidence on screen. It can never prejudge it. Vidor is superior to Milestone' (1996: 119). There are two related problems. First, there is no reason why a 'pictorial image' should be considered to be less significant than a 'dramatic image'. Second, these scenes are examined out of context with the remainder of each of the films. Sarris does not demonstrate that a pictorial approach to the scene is inappropriate in the context of the film. *All Quiet on the Western Front* clearly relies heavily on *The Big Parade*. The similarities between the films, in conjunction with the depiction of the differ-

... as does Paul (Lew Ayres) in *All Quiet on the Western Front* (1930)

ent sides in the war, introduce a complexity in the readings of the two films that is not in either by itself. Moreover, with only five years separating these two films, the latter film's clear intertextual reference to *The Big Parade* is itself based on an authorial decision (although not necessarily Milestone's). Sarris intends his auteur theory as a film historiography, but clearly there are problems with this approach. Examining these two films as autonomous texts requires the auteur critic to disconnect the films from their exhibition contexts. There are better models of film criticism and historiography.

Pauline Kael was the most vociferous detractor of auteur criticism and theory. Her 1963 essay 'Circles and Squares' is a polemical assault on Sarris's 'Notes on the Auteur Theory in 1962'. Kael makes a number of substantial charges against auteur criticism, most significantly that it changes the role of the critic from evaluating films to sifting films through a formula, and a bad formula at that. Sarris develops his argument using three metaphorical circles that identify the conceptual ranges required to evaluate a director via the auteur theory: 'the outer circle as technique; the middle circle, personal style; and the inner circle, interior meaning' (1985: 538). Kael confronts each of these 'circles' in turn. Why, she asks, should a great director also need technical competence to be considered a great director? Sarris suggests that 'if a director has no technical competence, no elementary flair for the cinema, he is automatically cast out from the pantheon of directors' (1985: 537). This may seem sensible, and nobody is suggesting that directors should not have good technological knowledge of film production, but it imposes a criterion that has no clear aesthetic justification. One of the main roles of a director is to direct those with the relevant technical competencies. If criteria for a director are required, should they not focus on a well-developed sense of aesthetic judgement? With something like this in mind Kael very quickly offers Sarris a counterexample:

> It is doubtful if Antonioni could handle a routine directorial assign-
> ment of the type at which John Struges is so proficient (*Escape*

Stylistic framing in *L'Avventura* (1960)

from Fort Bravo or *Bad Day at Black Rock*), but surely Antonioni's
L'Avventura is the work of a great director.[12] (1985: 544)

Sarris's image of the auteur is weighted towards American cinema and classical narrative construction. Being a European 'art film director', Antonioni
is simply outwith Sarris's methodological limits. If the question of authorship was about directorial abilities within various modes of production,
then there may be a reason to accept Sarris's distinction. Sarris does not
premise his view about technical competency on modes of production,
though, so it is reasonable to ask with Kael why technical competency
should be a criterion. Yet it is difficult to overestimate the significance that
films like *L'Avventura* (1960), *Red Desert* (1964), *Blowup* (1966) and *The
Passenger* (1975) have had on cinema, including American cinema. The
problem Kael identifies is that too many critical judgements are based in
personal preference. Kael instead does not prescribe that films must be
'art', however defined, but that they are successful within their own criteria. If an adventure film entertains, who is to say it is bad? The skill of the
critic rests in being able to recognise whether a film is successful on its
own terms, not on the terms prescribed by the critic.

Kael next asks, in response to Sarris's middle circle, why should
'distinguishability of personality' (1985: 545; emphasis in original) be
a relevant criterion? If spectators examine films for marks of the directors' personalities, there likely isn't much else in the films to maintain
their attentions. Further, this search for the truly gifted directors occurs
only with a critical gloss. It requires the critic to distinguish the artistic
attributes of a director from all the properties of a film. Even if this could be
achieved, and Victor Perkins gives good reason to indicate that this will be
a remarkably difficult task (see 1972: 158–86),[13] the threshold between the
auteur and the *metteur-en-scène* is nevertheless arbitrary. Further, once
this threshold has been crossed, then the auteur's weak films are forgiven
on the strength of the stronger ones. Auteur critics never tire of stating that
the worst efforts of an auteur are better than the best efforts of a hack.
Kael rightly asks on what grounds such an assertion can be defended, and
notes that it necessarily surrenders the critic's responsibility to aesthetic
judgement, since the evaluation of a work is made primarily on form rather
than merit. Peter Wollen (2003), discussing Michael Curtiz, demonstrates
that the *critical genius* of the auteur critic is not sufficient for the task of

establishing who is and is not an auteur, and that real graft is required to research production histories and understand the division of labour in any given production. He argues persuasively that auteur critics have been unnecessarily harsh on Curtiz. Without such graft, Kael notes, the critic can rely only on 'mystical insight' to make judgements. She concludes that Sarris's middle circle casts certain directors as idealised essences 'separated from all the life that has formed them and to which they try to give expression' (1985: 548).

Kael's final arguments address Sarris's inner circle, which suggests that a director must be in conflict with the story material. She characterises auteurists views, as conveyed by Sarris, eloquently:

> Their ideal auteur is the man who signs a long-term contract, directs any script that's handed to him, and expresses himself by shoving bits of style up the crevasses of the plots. If his 'style' is in conflict with the story line or subject matter, so much the better – more chance for tension. (1985: 548–9)

In good dialectical fashion, this tension between the 'director's personality and his material' produces 'interior meaning', Sarris maintains (1985: 538). Despite this, he struggles to define what 'interior meaning' means, except that it is something ineffable. Kael rightly draws attention to this problem and begs a distinction between 'interior meaning' and 'meaning' (1985: 542). Presumably there is no distinction, since there is no 'external meaning' against which 'interior meaning' can be defined. Instead, she suggests that for Sarris the term 'interior meaning' betrays the mystique of auteur criticism: 'what those in the know know' (1985: 552). In cabalistic tradition they mystify interpretation behind a theory of artists rather than use criticism to elaborate publicly the meanings and significances of films. Kael asks why not just celebrate films that people enjoy, regardless how they came about. This ultimately is Kael's central criticism: auteur theory is a recipe for avoiding robust criticism.

In the late 1960s auteur criticism changed, taking on the methodologies of structuralism and then poststructuralism as responses to the methodological limitations of auteur criticism. Wollen suggests that 'the auteur theory has survived despite all the hallucinating critical extravaganzas which it has fathered. It has survived because it is indispensable' (1972: 79–80). It is indispensable because it permits a certain type of knowledge about film. Kael's approach to criticism is predominantly textual. Even if the names of the people behind the production were unknown, a film could and should still be read as a text. However, any text may mask themes and meanings that can only be recognised by a critic with sufficient knowledge of the auteur's work to recognise repeated motifs and interpret their significance across the films. Wollen attributes this 'auteur-structuralism' to Geoffrey Nowell-Smith. Nowell-Smith, in his introduction to his book *Luchino Visconti*, posits that

> the purpose of criticism becomes therefore to uncover behind the superficial contrasts of subject and treatment a structural hard core of basic and often recondite motifs. The pattern formed by these motifs, which may be stylistic or thematic, is what gives an author's work its peculiar structure, both defining it internally and distinguishing one body of work from another. (2003: 10–11)

In *Signs and Meanings in the Cinema* (1972) Wollen quotes Nowell-Smith approvingly, but omits his caveats.[14] Nowell-Smith adds that a structuralist approach to criticism has two main limitations: 'one is the possibility of an author's work changing over time and of the structure being variable and not consistent; the other is the importance of the non-thematic subject matter and of sub-stylistic features of the visual treatment' (2003: 11). Nowell-Smith argues that subsequently some directors may be appropriate for structuralist criticism, but Visconti, given the breadth of his film styles and topics, is not among them.

Informed by structural anthropology and semiotics, auteur structuralism aimed to found film criticism on a rigorous methodology with an air of science about it. Rather than looking for the artist's personality across a series of texts, structuralism 'in fact posited two structures – a structure of sameness and generality and a counter structure of difference and singularity' (Wollen 1996: 2). In his book *Horizons West* (2004), Jim Kitses utilises this approach, but not strictly as an authorial or textual concern. He is interested in how the genre of the western provides a framework within which certain auteurs developed. This approach has merit if only for its methodology that sees authorship within the historical development of a genre and production environment. Structural motifs may develop specific idiosyncrasies in the hands of a certain director and her or his collaborators, but the motifs themselves are generally common to anyone working in the genre. In order to understand what made John Ford a great director, he argues, one must also understand what the genre of the western offered Ford that he was able to utilise so effectively.[15] In other words, if Ford can be analysed through the study of myth, it is only because he restates established myths in his films in the form of the genre of the western.

This shift from artist to structure has its roots in the writings of Claude Lévi-Strauss and Vladimir Propp. Despite differences in their theories, they share the notion that basic story elements, or 'mythemes', repeat across narratives. Lévi-Strauss makes clear that for the study of myths, the origins of myths are irrelevant – myths lack authoritative versions against which iterations of the story can be compared. Instead, all incarnations of mythemes form part of an ideal archetype or metastory (1981: 135). Wollen notes that this should not be interpreted simply as a methodology of repeated motifs. 'There is a danger, as Lévi-Strauss has pointed out, that by simply noting and mapping resemblances, all the texts which are studied (whether Russian fairy-tales or American movies) will be reduced to one, abstract and impoverished' (1972: 93). To be appropriately structuralist, criticism should also take into account 'differential elements', examining the *antinomies* within and between films (Wollen 1972: 94). Wollen applies this method to authorship instead of stories and folklore. By rooting his auteur theory in structure rather than expression, Wollen, who according to Brian Henderson offers the 'purest' analysis of auteur structuralism (see 1981: 175–6), aims to construct a theory that can be applied to any film, rather than just art cinema and its Romantic concept of 'expression and individual vision':

> Any film ... is a network of different statements, crossing and contradicting each other, elaborated into a final 'coherent' version. Like a dream, the film the spectator sees is, so to speak, the 'film façade', the end-product of 'secondary revision', which hides and masks the process which remains latent in the film 'unconscious' ... It is this structure which *auteur* analysis disengages from the film. (1972: 167; emphasis in original)

In 1973, both Charles Eckert (2008) and Brian Henderson (1981) argued independently that Wollen's approach is inherently confused and contend there is a fundamental difference between Lévi-Strauss's project and Wollen's auteur structuralism. Henderson reminds us that 'myths have no origins, no centres, no subjects and no authors' (1981: 176). The auteur theory proposes precisely the opposite, looking for the subject at the centre of any given film project. To have any hope of developing a sound theory, Henderson insists, Wollen needs to explain how subjects produce structures and how these can be analysed in the way that myths are analysed. This Wollen fails to do (see Henderson 1981: 176–7).

In his 1972 edition of *Signs and Meaning in the Cinema*, Wollen notes that the 1969 edition of his book was written at the beginning of a transitional period in film aesthetics and criticism, and that his arguments then presumed an instrumental use of language, including the associated notions of intention, content and a singular reading of any text (1972: 155–60). By 1972 his understanding of texts had changed, reflecting the critique of structuralism that had erupted in France in the late 1960s:

> The text is no longer a transparent medium ... It is open rather than closed; multiple rather than singular; productive rather than exhaustive. Although it is produced by an individual, the author, it does not simply represent or express the author's ideas, but exists in its own right. (1972: 163)

Rejecting an author's authority over a text, Wollen cannot retain a straightforward reference to the director and her or his conscious intentions. Nevertheless, he aims to retain a form of authorship theory, so theories that abandon authorship entirely are not options.[16] Instead, he combines two solutions. First, he shifts attention from the director's conscious efforts to her or his unconscious preoccupations. These are the structures that the auteur structuralist will be tasked with tracing. Second, since the text cannot be equated to the director's conscious ideas, and it exists independent of the conditions of its material construction, it would be wrong to associate interpretations of the text with the director. To resolve this need to name the entity whose unconscious shaped the text, and to separate the text from authorial intention and ownership, Wollen opts for what appears to be Michel Foucault's notion of an 'author function', a named discourse stemming from the reception of a text but disconnected from authorial intention.[17]

The structure is associated with a single director, an individual, not because he has played the role of the artist, expressing himself or his vision of the film, but because it is through the force of his preoccupations that an unconscious, unintended meaning can be decoded in the film. Auteur analysis does not consist of retracing a film to its origins, to its creative source. It consists of tracing a structure (not a message) within a work, which can then *post factum* be assigned to an individual, the director, on empirical grounds. It is wrong, in the name of a denial of the traditional idea of creative subjectivity, to deny any status to individuals at all. But Fuller or Hawks or Hitchcock, the directors, are quite separate from 'Fuller' or 'Hawks' or 'Hitchcock', the structures named after them, and should not be methodologically confused. (1972: 167–8)

Wollen's 1972 revision is problematic. To begin with he does not state clearly what he means by 'unconscious' and the specific analysis of his named structures. Nowell-Smith finds Wollen's suggestion appealing if 'unconscious' is used in a generic sense, as in one is not fully aware of one's actions or consequences, but is sceptical of the term if it is used technically in the psychoanalytical sense, since 'it is more likely to be in the form of a repeating symptom than of a principle of coherence' (2003: 220–1). The colloquial or generic notion of the unconscious will not work for Wollen. Working through a question asked by Nowell-Smith indicates why: 'In what way unconscious? In the way one is unconscious of simple motor activity such as breathing? Or unconscious of the rules of language?' (2003: 220). Nowell-Smith's analogy is apt, since it focuses on the distinction between expression and the system within which an expression can be structured. Looking closely at this analogy, it seems that unconscious structures can hardly be of much critical importance, once we consider comparatively the relative significance of the statements we express consciously against our lack of awareness of the grammatical rules that we use in making them. These generically 'unconscious' elements are essentially part of our conscious expression, just as grammatical usage is part of our ordinary expression.[18] Such a colloquial notion of unconscious would make any anti-intentionalist theory like Wollen's questionable, at least as far as the theory was premised on the notion of the unconscious. If, however, Wollen advocates a technical notion of the unconscious, then some explanation is warranted indicating how structures such as Ford's 'garden versus wilderness, plough-share versus sabre, settler versus nomad ...' are unconscious rather than conscious.[19] Coupled with an empirical connection back to the director of a film, this approach seems to resurrect the Romantic notion of the author, this time as an unconscious, rather than conscious genius.[20]

At *Cahiers du cinéma*, auteur criticism did not disappear, but as in the UK shifted towards structuralism and poststructuralism following the protests and general strike of 1968. While the British structuralists were engaged in a predominantly textual project, the *Cahiers du cinéma* group was more interested in ideology. As Bill Nichols notes, two essays in particular establish *Cahiers du cinéma*'s new approach. Jean-Luc Comolli and Jean Narboni published their methodological statement in 'Cinema/Ideology/Criticism', in *Cahiers du cinéma* 216 (1969). The essay 'John Ford's *Young Mr. Lincoln*', a collective text by the editorial board of the journal, followed in issue 223 (1970). The latter essay functions as an exemplar of Comolli and Narboni's method, especially regarding self-critical films (or 'category (e)' films, as itemised in Comolli and Narboni's essay).[21] In contrast to *Cahiers du cinéma*'s auteur criticism, these essays establish clearly a methodology and criteria for reading and evaluating films. This mode of criticism abandons examining film for its artistry or its combination of repetition and variation. Instead, the editors argue, it should embark on a

> process of active reading ... to make [the films] say what they have to say *within* what they leave unsaid, to reveal their constituent lacks; these are neither faults in the work ... nor a deception on the part of the author ... they are *structuring absences*, always displaced – an overdetermination which is the only possible basis from which these discourses could be realised, the unsaid included in the said and necessary to its constitution. (*Cahiers du cinéma* 1976: 496; emphasis in original)

This approach is notable for (1) its shift towards a Marxist-Freudian framework that moves beyond the mere unconscious of the individual, and (2) its poststructural method of focusing on reading rather than the elocutionary force of an originating auteur. It is fundamentally political. Comolli and Narboni note that film is embedded in economics and contend that it is

SHORT CUTS

therefore determined by capitalist ideology. Further, since reality is itself ideological, they argue, cinema, being a photographic medium, captures the prevailing ideology and reflects it back on society. 'What the camera in fact registers is the vague, unformulated, untheorised, unthought-out world of the dominant ideology' (1976: 24–5). Many films will simply and uncritically reflect that ideology, but not all films. Critical attention should be focused on locating those films that if read 'obliquely', or 'symptomatically', will demonstrate themselves as being 'riddled with cracks: it is splitting under an internal tension which is simply not there in an ideologically innocuous film' (Comolli & Narboni 1976: 27). Known occasionally as 'category (e) films', these films offer a critique of capitalist ideology while at the same time appearing to repeat it. Interestingly this shift in critical method did not shift the paradigm of film texts valorised by *Cahiers du cinéma*. Hitchcock, Ford, Jean Renoir, Carl Theodor Dreyer, Roberto Rossellini and Josef von Sternberg all retained their auteur status and films directed by Ford and Hitchcock in particular proved useful for exemplifying this new approach to criticism.

In their remarkably attentive analysis of *Young Mr. Lincoln* (1939), the *Cahiers du cinéma* editors locate the film's critique of ideology within Ford's oeuvre, the American film industry and the conditions of the Unites States, especially the economic conditions that resulted from both capitalism and the Depression. By underscoring their analysis with a psychoanalytical-Marxist critique of economics and ideology, the *Cahiers du cinéma* editors seem to rely on the meta-language that they explicitly deny adopting. This mode of criticism is more a symptom of its historical context than the objective approach for identifying politically progressive films within a capitalist film industry that the editors set out to achieve. The main shortcoming of the approach is it determines the scope of the analyses and the conditions that establish a critique of ideology. For instance, the *Cahiers du cinéma* editors map the resemblances between the Lincoln and Clay families (for much of the film both lack a father) and the fact that Lincoln studies law (initiated by a book he receives from the Clays) onto Freud's notion of 'Law of the Father'. Lincoln represents the law in the film, but gains his authority not from the father, but from the mother – the law is simultaneously authoritative and castrating, and it is the latter, the editors argue, that undercuts the bourgeois ideology of the former.[22] Gaining authority from the mother rather than the father is not politically transgressive, nor does it represent cracks or instabilities in the capitalist ideology that enabled the film to be produced. This reading is only transgressive within the bounds of an ideologically informed psychoanalysis. By attending to these 'ruptures', the *Cahiers du cinéma* editors, David Bordwell notes, characterise the auteur as 'a subversive textual force rather than a visionary individual' (1989: 86). The director does not consciously structure these ruptures, or secret messages, into the work; they appear as a result of overdeterminations. It is as if Ford could not help but produce such an ideologically contradictory text.[23]

Despite these problems, the approach epitomised by the editors' analysis of *Young Mr. Lincoln* had two significant consequences for film criticism and the study of film authorship. First, as Bordwell indicates, it encouraged a degree of detail in film analysis that had been rarely practised previously (1989: 86). Second, it shifted the investigation of authorship away from intention towards reception.[24] Since language is neither owned nor fixed by any author, the editors note, neither the spectator nor the text are fixed points in the reading process. Meaning is beyond the author's control. The notion of 'action reading' that the editors endorse casts both the text and the spectator in the process of *becoming*. No reading will ever be conclusive. This has an important impact on the understanding of authorship. The author loses her or his place as the authority of a text, which problematises the very notion of authorship. This shift is largely indebted to the work of Jacques Derrida and his notions of *différance* and of the supplement, whereby the 'signified' of a signifier is substituted by another signifier (Derrida 1973: 88–9). These issues will be dealt with in greater detail in the next chapter.[25] For our purposes here, though, the important concerns are that neither the author nor the text is seen as an authority over meaning, and that the emphasis has been shifted to the reader of the text. Derrida's ideas underscore this shift in criticism and conceptions of authorship, but his arguments have not been a dominating presence in film theory and criticism. Thus, where *Cahiers du cinéma* had been at the forefront of celebrating certain directors as artists of the cinema, with this text on *Young Mr. Lincoln* the editors undermine this project. They do not deny Ford's skill as a filmmaker, but consider the meaning of the film from the framework of reception and the notion of overdetermination. Overdetermination pins multiple causes to a single effect. No longer is Ford seen as the sole originator of the film, but one among a number of causes. The film sits as a node within a broader, unstable semantic and aesthetic matrix.

Within a short period of time in French film criticism, the concept of the author had changed dramatically. Astruc's 1948 proclamation of '*caméra-stylo*' and the director as cinematic writer was superseded in the late 1960s by Derrida's *écriture* (writing), which resists the notion of finality and solidity in signification. It minimises the role of the writer and emphasises the role of the reader as a location of meaning production. This radically alters the notion of the author as Romantic genius. The author, whether in literature or in film, is no longer separated from society, but with the reader is deeply embedded within the dynamics of language, representation and ideology. Moreover, but undermining the instrumental use of language, poststructuralists questioned the very control that this ideologically embedded author has. A critical project that aimed to venerate those directors that somehow managed to repeatedly produce films that were distinguishable from the standard commercial entertainment ended up as a theoretical project that questioned the very capacities of authorship through both ideology's capacity to determine the social subject and the instability of language and representation. The winner of this project was not the director, but the critic that managed to legitimise the act of reading at the expense of the notion of the author. In the next chapter I will examine the logic, justification and implications of this development.

2   AUTHORSHIP AND RECEPTION

The shift discussed in the previous chapter from auteur criticism, to the recurrent thematics of auteur structuralism, and the ideological overdeterminations of what can problematically be called auteur poststructuralism, involved a transition from intentionalist to anti-intentionalist theories. Put simply, intentionalists maintain that the author's intent is essential for interpreting a work, and anti-intentionalists that the author's intentions have no bearing on a work's meaning once it is in circulation. Anti-intentionalists maintain that texts have 'textual meanings' – they simply mean what they mean. Textual meanings will be either more or less stable depending if one views language as more or less stable respectively. In this chapter I will examine anti-intentionalist literary theories and how they have affected understandings of film authorship. This shift to anti-intentionalism in film theory since the late 1960s is founded largely in French philosophy and literary theory, and significantly in the work of Jacques Derrida. Despite Derrida's centrality in poststructuralist literary theory, his work has had limited direct influence on film studies, as Peter Brunette and David Wills note (1989: 3). Instead, the arguments of Roland Barthes and Michel Foucault proved more utilitarian for theories of film authorship that aimed to empower the reader against the semantic tyranny of the author. Poststructuralism is not the only source of anti-intentionalism in theories of film authorship. W. K. Wimsatt and Monroe Beardsley epitomised the formalist approach of American New Criticism that established meaning as a textual concern. Wayne Booth, influenced by both Chicago School Criticism and New Criticism,[1] developed an analysis of authorship that explored the middle ground between intentionalism and anti-intentionalism. Booth's arguments have had a lasting influence on theories of film narration and authorship informed by cognitive psychology and analytical philosophy. Anti-intentional theories of authorship, especially those that employ what I call an 'author surrogate' (author function, implied author, ideal author and so forth), have much to recommend them. They do not require the critic to guess what is in the head of the author or perform an act of 'psychobiography'. They easily accommodate collective authorship, and enable the reader as a producer of meaning. They do so, I will argue, at the cost of a serious tautology. Author surrogate theories can be valuable, but, I aim to demonstrate, they do not negate concerns for authors' intentions. The notion of an author surrogate makes sense only in its relationship with the empirical author(s).

Jacques Derrida is arguably the most important and influential of the poststructuralist literary theorists. He maintains that language is unstable because signs do not retain direct and permanent correlations between signifiers and signifieds. David B. Allison, in his 'Translator's Introduction' to Derrida's *Speech and Phenomena* (1973), usefully summarises Derrida's positions, noting that meaning is dependent

> upon nonpresent elements. Meaning can never be isolated or held in abstraction from its context, e.g., its linguistic, semiotic or historical context. Each such context, for example, is a system of references, a system of signifiers, whose function and reality point beyond the present … We can only assemble and recall the traces of what went before; we stand within language, not outside it. (1973: xxxviii)

These contexts imbue language and perpetually reshape it. Consequently, language constantly revises the very concepts we think about. There is no ideal place outside of language that will allow an objective analysis of any linguistic expression, and therefore no ideal meaning behind any expression, since expressions have a variety of contexts, including those of writing and reading. Derrida does not conclude there. An expression refers also to the act of expression, but this reference will always be imperfect, since the act of expression is gone the moment it has been performed.

Therefore, neither the author nor the author's meaning is fully recoverable through reading. The image of an author that a reader constructs is a *supplement* for the real author and is always unstable. In *Speech and Phenomena*, Derrida puts it as follows: 'My death is structurally necessary to the pronouncing of the *I*' (1973: 96; emphasis in original). The act of writing separates the 'I' of the text from the person who wrote. The 'I' of the text is a signifier for that 'I' that existed at the point of writing, but that can never be recovered (see 1973: 88–104; 1976: 141–64).[2] Derrida insists that intention is important for writing, and therefore reading a text, but that intention itself is a sign and not fully available to the reader. Seán Burke offers the following summary: 'critical production therefore consists in a redoubling of the intentional structure and the warring play of signification by which intention is destabilised' (1995a: 68–9).

Instead, Roland Barthes' 1967 essay 'The Death of the Author' (see 1977a) and Michel Foucault's 1969 essay 'What is an Author?' (see 1984) provided more digestible and usable arguments in film theory. Although Barthes and Foucault generally agree with Derrida's analysis of language, they depart from his views on intention and authorship. Barthes maintains that as a result of the instability of language, language is uncontainable and speaks *through* writers (what he calls 'modern scriptors'). The only location of meaning is the point of reception, and even this is ephemeral. Foucault generally accepts Barthes' analysis but does not dismiss the reader's impression of authorial voices in texts. These impressions are indications of a discourse rather than authorial intention. Barthes and Foucault were not the first theorists to challenge authorial intention. Notably, W. K. Wimsatt and Monroe Beardsley argued in their seminal 1946 essay 'The Intentional Fallacy' that authorial intention governs writing, but plays no privileged role in the interpretation of texts. 'The design or intention of the author is neither available nor desirable as a standard for judging the success of a work of literary art' (1982: 3). Film theorists with an interest in ideology gravitated to Barthes' and Foucault's anti-intentionalism. Since language structured individuals and was inherently ideological, these arguments helped to support analyses of films that saw readers and spectators as subjects of texts. Wimsatt and Beardsley's views, largely through their influence on Wayne Booth, underscore approaches to film criticism that view language and film as intelligible systems that have no inherent ideological properties. Individuals are not subjects of language, but use language to communicate. Language evolves and meaning varies with usage, but despite this, expressions are largely stable and intelligible. If a novel or film has an ideological perspective, it is a function of the meaning of the text rather than the nature of language or representation. Although both poststructuralists and New Critics reject authorial intention, their reasons for doing so are very different and incompatible with each other.[3]

Despite this incompatibility, Wimsatt and Beardsley's notion of 'the intentional fallacy' has become a tacit perspective underscoring a range of anti-intentionalist arguments about film authorship. Subsequently it deserves a few brief comments here. The object of Wimsatt and Beardsley's interest is poetry. The question I wish to consider is whether their argument can apply to film also. Wimsatt and Beardsley only reject interpretation as a criterion for criticism, insisting that poems are nevertheless intentionally produced. Poems do not

> come into existence by accident. The words of a poem, as Professor Stoll has remarked, come out of a head, not out of a hat. Yet to insist on the designing intellect as a *cause* of a poem is not to grant the design or intention as a *standard* by which the critic is to judge the worth of a poet's performance. (1982: 4; emphasis in original)

To apply 'the intentional fallacy' to film, all one needs to demonstrate is that film is analogous to, or sufficiently like poetry in the right sort of ways. Fortunately we need not provide a definition of poetry, only consider what type of acts of writing Wimsatt and Beardsley exclude from their argument. Whatever a poem is, it is distinct from 'practical messages'. Practical messages require the recognition of intention in order to be understood. A poem functions differently:

> The poem belongs to the public. It is embodied in language, the peculiar possession of the public, and it is about the human being, an object of public knowledge. What is said about the poem is subject to the same scrutiny as any statement in linguistics or in the general science of psychology. (1982: 5)

When discussing whether the intentional fallacy applies to film, clearly we cannot include all film, just as poetry excludes some uses of language.

A training film, like 'how to wire a plug' must be read through its intention – in this case to educate how to safely do a basic electrical repair. The film cannot be read as a metaphor about something like conformity because that was not the intention behind its production. If Wimsatt and Beardsley's intentional fallacy applies to film, it can only therefore apply to those films that have a mode of abstract expression, such as fictional, experimental and a range of documentary films.[4] When summoning the 'intentional fallacy', critics usually have these types of film in mind.

Wimsatt and Beardsley point out that the culture and language that poems are composed in are public, which means that the standards for interpreting poetry are also public. Poets employ a number of aesthetic strategies such as rhythm, repetition, phrasing, rhyme, allusion, conventional word usage and the poet's previous word usage to establish the tonal, affective and semantic dimensions of the poem. We can understand a specific poem because we understand how poems function and have experience reading other poems. Film similarly has capacities such as rhythm, allusion, phrasing and framing, which form part of its public culture. Knowledge of film culture aids the interpretation of any individual film. Cultural knowledge forms only part of Wimsatt and Beardsley's argument, though. Poems are composed in language. Herein lies a problem for film. A language has a grammar that establishes the conditions for sense and governs usage. Films have conventions, but no grammar.[5] Genres are composed of conventions, but these can generally be ignored in any instance and the film can still be interpreted and remain part of the genre. A film can be produced and read independent of any convention. Poems that abandon grammatical rules are still read against the background of grammar that they have abandoned. Language, in semiotic terms, is completely arbitrary. Film is different because the image is motivated by the object it depicts. The word 'tree' has an inherent meaning whereas a photograph or film of a tree does not. In practice, we rarely even have pictures of just trees, but trees in forests or fields. The meaning comes from the context. The title 'Poplar', or 'Deforestation', or the juxtaposition of the image with an image of a chainsaw, plough or cityscape will all affect the understanding one has of the image. The image of the tree and the plough can make sense in either order, with any length shot, from any angle, even though the specific sense of the two shots will likely differ with each variation. No *rules* govern composition in pictures, but they do in language. 'Green tree' makes sense because it conforms to the order of adjectives and nouns. 'Tree green' does not make sense because it disobeys this rule. Proponents of Christian Metz's 'General Table of the Large Syntagmatic Category of the Image-Track' (see 1991: 146) may contest that Metz has demonstrated that film has a grammar. Metz's categories are, though, descriptive categories of conventions of classical film construction, not rules. Metz is correct when he states that the *fact that must be understood is that films are understood*' (1991: 145; emphasis in original). This truism does not justify elevating conventions to a grammar. The rules of language are essential for Wimsatt and Beardsely because they enable, without recourse to the author's intentions, interpretation even when cultural understandings fail.

Film works differently. As the cultural familiarity of certain types of film practice diminishes, so does the capacity to understand these films without recourse to intention. *High Noon* (1952) is understandable because it relies extensively on the genre of the western and star actors. *Dog Star Man* (1961–1964) and *Reassemblage* (1983) are also understandable, but far more problematic for the uninitiated and uninformed spectator. The lack of a grammar is compounded by limited filmic conventions. To make sense of films such as these, spectators must supplement whatever conventions they can recognise with inference: 'why compose this image in this way?' This inference is an attempt to grapple with intention. The difference between *High Noon* and *Dog Star Man* is that the former is strongly conventional and the latter weakly conventional. Both share the problem that the limits of convention mark the limits of public standards for interpretation, leaving only the private realm of intention as a guide. I am not arguing that 'the intentional fallacy' *cannot* apply to film, only that the absence of a grammar in film eliminates a central public resource for the interpretation of film. Film does not seem sufficiently like language, in the right sort of ways, to accommodate 'the intentional fallacy'. One apparent option is to abandon the notion of objective interpretation. This option, however, abandons the central principle of 'the intentional fallacy'. Meaning on this account is no longer publicly available, but privately resident in each reader.

Barthes' and Foucault's versions of anti-intentionalism inspired French and British critics and theorists from the late 1960s onwards. They share with Wimsatt and Beardsley a belief that interpretation cannot be rooted in or informed by the biography of the author. In 'The Death of the Author', Barthes takes this a step further and rejects the very notion of authorial intention. He does not deny that some individual is, and always has been, responsible for making marks on a page, but this does not constitute writing a *text*. A text is constituted in language and is therefore beyond the capacity of any individual to control. Language speaks through subjects, according to Barthes, not the other way around: a 'text is not a line of words releasing a single "theological" meaning (the "message" of the Author-God), but a multi-dimensional space in which a variety of writings, none of them original, blend and clash' (1977a: 146). The very notion of an author, he contends, is a historical anomaly, appearing in the Middle Ages 'with English empiricism, French rationalism and the personal faith of the reformation [that] discovered the prestige of the individual' (1977a: 142–3). The reader becomes the point of coherency, but even here meaning is not ultimately fixed. Each act of reading constitutes a new meaning.

There are (at least) two basic problems with Barthes' argument. First, his separation of 'writing' from intention denaturalises language. If it no longer enables expression or communication, what function does language have? An endless play of quotations and signs is a rather trivial use for such an important and useful human capacity. Peter Lamarque adds further that to separate intention from writing would be like

> trying to hear a Mozart symphony as a mere string of unstructured sound ... To use language as meaningful discourse is to perform speech acts; to understand discourse is, minimally, to grasp what speech acts are performed. Barthes' view of *écriture* and texts tries to abstract language from the very function that gives it life. (2002: 90)

Second, as Lamarque protests further, why should the proliferation of meanings in reading be preferable to limitations on meaning? Barthes' desire to escape the determinacy of a text is based on a fictitious notion of 'some bullying authoritarian author' (Lamarque 2002: 91). The result is a relativistic view of language 'as a limitless and unrestricted source of connotation and allusion' (ibid.). By locating meaning in the reader Barthes shifts from a Romantic conception of the author to a Romantic conception of language and of the reader, and as a consequence makes language meaningless because of its infinite variability in the reader.

Meaning becomes ephemeral and purely subjective, confounding the public aspects of language that makes communication possible.

The main casualty of this reformulation of language is the concept of expression, which Barthes clearly delineates from inscription. Inscription is simply the process of making marks, whereas expression is the act of relating innately individual things such as thoughts and passions. When writing, one inscribes not one's expressions, Barthes argues, but language. For this reason he refers to the modern writer as a 'modern scriptor':

> Having buried the Author, the modern scriptor can thus no longer believe, as according to the pathetic view of his predecessors, that this hand is too slow for his thought or passion and that consequently, making a law of necessity, he must emphasise this delay and indefinitely 'polish' his form. For him, on the contrary, the hand, cut off from any voice, borne by a pure gesture of inscription (and not of expression), traces a field without origin – or which, at least, has no other origin than language itself, language which ceaselessly calls into question all origins. (1977a: 146)

This argument found a receptive audience, Burke notes, precisely because its iconoclasm and anti-authoritarianism resonated with the spirit of the 1968 demonstrations. Further, it 'quite clearly [references] "The Death of God" as heralded by The Madman in Nietzsche's *The Joyful Wisdom*' (Burke 1998: 23).[6] Barthes' 'Author-God' is, however, a bit of a 'straw God'. He can only make his case by proposing two types of language, one for the Author-God, the other for the modern scriptor. By proposing that under an Authored work there is a direct and unambiguous correlation between an Author's meaning and the critical reception of the work, he seems to be suggesting that in Authored works language functions like formal rather than natural language.[7] Formal languages, such as those used in various fields of logic, mathematics and computer science, are constructed languages that have rigid rules governing grammatical usage, syntax and the use and meaning of symbols. Because these rigid rules determine the construction of an expression, they also determine its meaning. Intention plays no role in interpretation because the single meaning of an expression can be read transparently from the construction of the expression. In contrast, English, French, Spanish, Dutch and so on, are natural languages. Although there are rules governing the use and meaning of symbols, grammar and syntax, these rules are not rigid. They evolve through usage and are meaningful within their contexts, including the contexts of the speaker/writer and listener/reader. 'You must give him credit' means very different things depending on the context, whether spoken between employees at a bank, or a journalist writing about a politician. Expressions in natural languages are open to interpretation in a way that expressions in formal languages are not. In order to kill off his 'Author-God', Barthes must first construct one. By construing the 'Author-God's' message as a 'line of words releasing a single "theological" meaning (Barthes 1977a: 146), he only allows this Author-God the scope of a formal language. From this he concludes that the '*explanation* of a work is always sought in the man or woman who produced it' (1977a: 143). To justify abandoning the Author as authority he construes biography and Authorial intention as systems for valid interpretation in Authored works. By then demonstrating that texts do not have singular meanings, he concludes that authors are not responsible for meaning. Even if some critics interpret texts as psychobiography, this does not imply literature ever functioned in the rigid manner Barthes suggests. By executing his Author-God, Barthes is able to conclude that

> a text is made of multiple writings, drawn from many cultures and entering into mutual relations of dialogue, parody, contestation, but there is one place where this multiplicity is focused and that place is the reader, not, as was hitherto said, the author. The reader is the space on which all the quotations that make up a writing are inscribed without any of them being lost; a text's unity lies not in its origin, but in its destination. (1977a: 148)

If this were accurate, then any combination of words and any grammatical structure, or lack of, would produce a unity in its destination. Such an escalation of meanings, located solely at the point of reception and at the expense of expression, would make language meaningless. Natural languages and their uses are simply neither locked down by rules and structures nor bereft of them.

To be fair, 'The Death of the Author' was not offered, dare I say intended, as a rigorous, analytical approach to authorship. Barthes published the essay in the iconoclastic and experimental American journal *Aspen* in

1967, as part of a collection of essays that aimed to subvert 'conventional ways of thinking about, of approaching or theorising, literature and art, particularly with respect to conventional oppositions of "high" art to low cultural values' (Bennett 2005: 14). The essay's function was to conceive reading as a productive activity. The perfectly welcome suggestion that each reader engages uniquely with a text does not, though, require the author's execution. Not only is it possible that authors and readers cohabit texts, it seems that it may be necessary.

Wayne Booth and Michel Foucault, the former writing a little before Barthes, the latter shortly after (1961 and 1969 respectively), have offered related but different solutions to this persistent need for the author. They both propose what I call 'author surrogate' theories. Both agree with other anti-intentionalists that the author does not retain authority over her or his work once it is released into the public domain, but do not accept that this licenses the complete abandonment of the notion of the author. Each then proposes that an 'impression' of an author appears during the act of reading. This sense of an author that the reader perceives is not the empirical author that wrote the text, but the voice of a fictional entity produced by the text. The theories differ in that Booth locates this author surrogate, 'the implied author', in each work, whereas Foucault maintains that these surrogates, or author functions, arise as discourses that span collections of works. We saw in the previous chapter that Peter Wollen adopted a strategy similar to Foucault's, with the exception that Foucault makes no connection back to the author's unconscious. Between Booth and Foucault, it is Foucault who has been more visible in film studies, but probably Booth whom has had the more prolonged and direct impact in the field.

Foucault's argument came to be seen, somewhat inaccurately, as a companion to Barthes' 'The Death of the Author' and associated with poststructuralism.[8] Foucault makes clear throughout his essay, 'What is an Author?', his distance from Barthes' notion of the author's death. He does not deny the author's death, but asserts that it is 'not enough … to repeat the empty affirmation that the author has disappeared' (1984: 105). He warns that the abandonment of the author for the interplay of signs will not produce the 'here and now' conception of language reception that Barthes aims to achieve:

> Giving writing a primal status seems to be a way of retranslating, in transcendental terms, both the theological affirmation of its sacred

character and the critical affirmation of its creative character. To admit that writing is, because of the very history that it made possible, subject to the text of oblivion and repressions, seems to represent, in transcendental terms, the religious principle of hidden meaning (which requires interpretation) and the critical principle of implicit significations, silent determinations, and obscured contents (which gives rise to commentary) [...]

This usage of the notion of writing runs the risk of maintaining the author's privileges under the protection of writing's *a priori* status: it keeps alive, in the grey light of neutralisation, the interplay of those representations that formed a particular image of the author. (1984: 104–5)

Subsequently, he maintains that 'it is not enough to declare that we should do without the writer (the author) and study the work itself. The word *work* and the unity that it designates are probably as problematic as the status of the author's individuality' (1984: 104; emphasis in original). Barthes' 1971 essay 'From Work to Text' would appear to be a response to this concern. In it he addresses some of the objections his previous essay provoked.

It is not that the Author may not 'come back' in the Text, in his text, but he then does so as a 'guest'. If he is a novelist, he is inscribed in the novel like one of his characters, figured in the carpet; no longer privileged, paternal, aletheological, his inscription is ludic. He becomes, as it were, a paper-author: his life is no longer the origin of his fictions but a fiction contributing to his work. (1977b: 161)

Barthes distinction between 'work' and 'text' is rather intricate in its detail, but despite this a thumbnail sketch is possible. The 'work' is that physical thing produced by a physical being. It is an object in space and time, 'occupying a part of the space of books (in a library for example)' (1977b: 156–7). The 'text' is not physical and it is not bound by a work. Many works can contribute to a single text. It is a network of signifiers that continue to refer outwards to other signifiers. Whereas the work is a closed, finite object, the text is infinite in its permutations. The work is the domain of the modern scriptor, the text that of the reader. The work is a material object to be produced and consumed, the text a field of play and pleasure.

In contrast, Foucault adopts a more analytical and historical approach. The disappearance of the author reveals for Foucault a space of discourse. Central to his argument is *his* notion of a 'work'. Foucault does not employ Barthes' distinction between 'work' and 'text'. He maintains the word 'work' is difficult to define precisely because it has been historically variable and dependent upon evaluative criteria. It is not sufficient to say something like 'authors produce *works* of literature'. While they do, they also produce writings that are not works of literature. Is a 'work' of literature the final, published work, or could drafts and notes be included, or even shopping lists? Similarly, is someone who is not considered to be an author capable of producing works? Can writings at one point in time not be considered works but later become works retrospectively if someone is later recognised as an author? The manner in which Foucault structures these questions suggests that to be an author is not simply to be a writer, but a writer of some quality writing at the right place and time. Historical dispositions to certain types of writing change. He asserts that a 'private letter may well have a signer – it does not have an author' (1984: 107–8). He suggests further that in the Middle Ages what we now call scientific texts were considered true only if signed with the name of a respected author. In the seventeenth and eighteenth centuries, this changed and scientific literature could be read as if produced anonymously (see Foucault 1984: 107–9). Lamarque calls this the 'Historicist Thesis' and rightly points out that Foucault is rather general in his analysis. Foucault fundamentally recasts what being an author entails.

> There is a slide ... in the text conception from the mere association of the text and author to the much fuller conception of a text as a classifiable work of a certain kind fulfilling a purpose, expressing a meaning and yielding a value. (Lamarque 2002: 82)

Authorship, on such an account, becomes not an act of writing, but the consequence of certain texts in history.

Barthes' notion of writing, *écriture*, is problematic because it risks reinscribing in language the Romantic mystifications that structuralist and poststructuralist literary theorists aim to confront. Foucault avoids this problem by distinguishing language from 'discourse'. 'Discourse' is a slippery term because it does not identify a clearly defined position in semiotics or linguistics. Crudely, discourses are related notions, concepts, aesthetics, practices or ideas that cohere, but are unstable and impermanent. They may disappear, combine, contradict, or evolve into other discourses. They may come about because of the work of an individual or of groups. While the ideas, concepts, aesthetics, practices or notions that constitute discourses may be intentional, discourses themselves are not. Through the process of cohering, discourses establish social boundaries, not prescriptively, but by the epistemological limits that discourses impose on thought and knowledge. A discourse has no set boundaries, and can be restricted to the literary output of one individual, Marx, for instance, or become a school of thought, such as Marxism. Discourse provides Foucault with a way to resolve his authorial puzzle about which acts of writing are authored. Writings like *Capital* (1867) and the notes that were written when composing it are associated with the name 'Marx', a shopping list written by Marx is not. Barthes proposes no criteria to prefer one act of writing to another. All language usage, in principle, is equivalent. Foucault's notion of discourse identifies aggregates of successful ideas. These aggregates do not appear out of nowhere, but are part of the history of ideas. The right idea at the right time takes hold and pulls together other related ideas. The author's name persists, Foucault insists, as the name of a discourse, not as an empirical source. In agreement with Barthes, Foucault maintains that the biography of the author has no bearing on the interpretation of the work. Contrary to Barthes, he does not then surrender meaning to the fluidity of language and relativism of reception, but instead situates it within discourse. This produces a middle ground between the rigidity of formal language and the mutability of an infinite field of quotations.

Foucault begins his analysis of authors' names by stating that a proper name 'is the equivalent of a description' (1984: 105). He suggests this is John Searle's argument. It is not. Searle states clearly that:

> The uniqueness and immense pragmatic convenience of proper names in our language lies precisely in the fact that they enable us to refer publicly to objects without being forced to raise issues and come to an agreement as to which descriptive characteristics exactly constitute the identity of the object. They function not as descriptions, but as pegs on which to hang descriptions. (1969: 172)

Foucault does proceed to make some gestures towards Searle's point – 'the proper name and the author's name are situated between the two poles of description and designation' (1984: 106) – but twists it to suit his purposes. Searle argues that a proper name becomes associated with descriptions, but that there are no necessary or sufficient descriptions required for a proper name to refer to an object or individual. 'It is not necessary that both [a speaker and hearer] should supply the same identifying description, provided only that their descriptions are in fact true of the same object' (Searle 1969: 171). Searle's concern is to understand the distinction between a reference and a description. Foucault instead uses this argument to indicate how the name of the author singles out a discourse. This is problematic, since he requires the same name to identify the individual and deny it at the same time. He argues that the name associated with a discourse functions in some ways like the name associated with an individual, but does not single out the name of an author:

> Hermes Trismegistus did not exist, nor did Hippocrates – in the sense that Balzac existed – but the fact that several texts have been placed under the same name indicates that there has been established among them a relationship of homogeneity, filiation, authentication of some texts by the use of the others, reciprocal explication, or concomitant utilisation. (1984: 107)

Hippocrates provides a good case to consider Foucault's position. Hippocrates existed, was an important medical practitioner and was at the centre of an important school of medicine. While many seminal medical texts were eventually published under the name of Hippocrates, it is not clear which he wrote and which other members of the school produced, either singly or collectively. Such an example gives Foucault cause to maintain that there is a distinction to be made between the name of an author and an individual's proper name. It does not matter that Hippocrates did not write all the works attributed to his name, because that name, as an author function, refers to a discourse rather than a biological individual. This use of the author's name, Foucault argues, 'manifests the appearance of a certain discursive set and indicates the status of this discourse within a society and culture' (1984: 107).

This approach, at first glance, seems sensible. However, his understanding of a proper name is suspect. He maintains that the proper name attached to the individual writer that produced a text can also become an authorial name demarcating a social discourse. Thus, there are two objects – a human individual and a discourse – related by a single name, such as 'Hippocrates'. His general point is clear enough: 'the author does not precede the works; he is a certain functional principle by which, in our culture, one limits, excludes and chooses' (1984: 118–9). The author's name, *pace* Barthes, 'is therefore the ideological figure by which one marks the manner in which we fear the proliferation of meaning' (1984: 119). Foucault does not adequately explain *how* this demarcation is established if the real and historical fact of the author is cut off from the author function. What is the relationship between the names of Hippocrates the person and 'Hippocrates' that demarcates a discourse? It seems sensible to assume there is some relationship, given the frequent similarity between the names of the historical author and the author function. Hippocrates may not be the best example to consider, though, because the name Hippocrates has become entirely confused with what we could call 'Hippocratic discourse'. The historical distance to the time of writing has obscured our ability to inquire into the writing of the texts. We simply lack the evidence to determine whether this coincident use of a name stems from a social approach to language and discourse, or simply a lack of evidence and information. A different example may help to clarify matters.

Foucault mentions that re-examinations of Marx's texts modify Marxism. It is difficult to argue with this assertion. Rather, the relevant question is 'why?' The key to this problem is located in the terminology. Marxism is a discourse, developed by and around the writings of Marx, and to some degree Friedrich Engels. The proper name 'Karl Marx' singles out an individual associated with a set of properties, such as one of the two individuals who wrote *The Communist Manifesto* (1848) and is buried in London. The proper name 'Marxism' singles out a collection of ideas, a discourse, that focuses on (amongst other things) a historical critique of capital and the value of human labour. In both cases the proper names function not as descriptions but refer to a set of descriptions possible of an object. One may object that the name 'Marxism' is descriptive of a discourse in a way that the name 'Karl Marx' is not of the person. This is a fair point. The proper name 'Marxism' singles out Marx as the main source of ideas in the discourse and may therefore seem like a description. Searle calls such examples 'degenerate proper names' (1969: 173). Seeming like a description and being a description are two different things. The name 'Marxism', as discourse, only picks out ideas by following the reference to Marx, and then to the ideas he expressed.[9] If the proper name 'Marx' is not a description, neither then, in any substantial way, is the degenerate proper name 'Marxism'. The author function makes no sense unless it refers back to an author or collection of authors, not as an authority, but as a progenitor. But if we need to consider authors and their expressions, there seems no need to impose the notion of an author function.

By separating authors from their expressions, both Barthes and Foucault depart from the legal understanding of authorship. Molly Nesbit, in her essay 'What Was an Author?' (1995), examines the history of copyright in French law. She raises a few key concerns that make clear the limitations of Foucault's historical gloss, and that refocus generic questions of authorship to account for authorship in film. French copyright law dates to 1793 and was generally unrevised until 1957.

> The law of 1793 gave authors privileges that ordinary men did not enjoy: The authors of every kind of writing, the composers of music, the painters and draughtsmen who have their paintings and drawings engraved, will enjoy the exclusive and lifetime right to sell, to have sold and to distribute their work in the territory of the Republic and to cede the same in toto or in part. (Georges Chabaud quoted in Nesbit 1995: 248)

Known as the *droits d'auteur*, these rights applied to a range of media and were indifferent to the aesthetic or intellectual quality of the works. Rather, as Nesbit notes, the interesting aspect of the law is that it separated cultural production from industrial production. While discourse may have been indifferent to certain authors, the law was not. Photography and film were not included in French copyright law until 1957, well after Astruc, Truffaut and the *Cahiers du cinéma* critics had proclaimed directors as auteurs. Cinema required 'special consideration', Nesbit notes, largely because of the collective and industrial methods of production. The revision in the law bestowed author's rights on directors, and in this way only served the *politiques des auteurs* that had been mounted during the 1950s by the *Cahiers du cinéma*, but it also gave rights to some of the other members of the film crew, notably to the writers and the composers, and it gave control over the finished work to the production company ... The modernisation of the law in 1957 began to undermine the old, clear distinction between culture and industry. (1995: 254)

By the time that the 1985 amendments to French copyright law had been established, industry had been incorporated into the copyright laws initially composed to protect the individual's right to exploit the products of her or his intellect and skills. For Nesbit, Foucault's analysis suffers from two significant weaknesses. He separates writers from authors through discourse formation, whereas in law an author remains an author as long as one retains her or his rights. Perhaps more importantly, Foucault neglects the importance of the market economy within which authorship circulates and which legally defines the author in the first place (see Nesbit 1995: 255–6).

Wayne Booth proposes an anti-intentionalist author surrogate theory that makes no distinction between writer and author, and maintains her or his presence as the source of the text. He begins from Wimsatt and Beardsley's 'intentional fallacy', but adds an 'implied author' to account for distinctions between the attitudes and beliefs presented by the text's authorial voice and the beliefs and attitudes held by the actual author. Reading fiction, he contends, involves engaging numerous voices: those of the characters, the narrator and the author. Booth argues that the authorial, as opposed to the narrative, voice of a literary narrative does not necessarily convey such things as the sincerity, seriousness or ideas of the actual individual that composed the work. Instead, the reader is presented with textually constructed versions of the author:

Our sense of the implied author includes not only the extractable meanings but also the moral and emotional content of each bit of action and suffering of all the characters. It includes, in short, the intuitive apprehension of a completed artistic whole; the chief value to which *this* implied author is committed, regardless of what

party his creator belongs to in real life, is that which is expressed
by the total form. (1991: 73–4; emphasis in original)

Echoing the New Critics, Booth indicates that the biography and intention
of the author are not relevant criteria for reading a work. As the author
writes, 'he creates not simply an ideal, impersonal "man in general" but
an implied version of himself' (1991: 70). This is not necessarily intentionally created, nor need it be the same in every novel written by the same
individual. Ultimately, therefore, it is the reader that constructs an image
of the author from her or his engagement with the text. Booth also retains a
place for actual readers outside the text, but constructs idealised versions
of them within the text. The implied reader therefore does not encapsulate
the actual reader. Simply put, the implied author corresponds with the
meanings the reader attributes to the author, and the 'implied or postulated reader' with the idealised understandings the author aims to convey
to the reader.[10] 'The most successful reading is one in which the created
selves, author and reader, can find complete agreement' (Booth 1991:
138). Booth separates actual from implied authors and readers because
he is adamant that an analysis of authorship and readership must account
for the author's and reader's actual beliefs and the way in which these
intersect the beliefs ascribed to the author and reader in the text. The
reader's position inscribed by the text may be one that the actual reader
fully accepts, tolerates, disagrees with but is willing to entertain, or refutes
and resists. It is this distinction between the implied and actual reader
that for Booth guards against Barthes' fear of theistic control over the
authored text. Reading for Booth entails an act of accepting a role offered
by an author and adapting it, not the process of being positioned by a text.
Booth's analysis thus sets up an interaction between the actual author
and reader through the performance of the surrogate roles of the implied
author and reader respectively.

Booth's and Foucault's author surrogate theories proved resilient in
film studies as they, to different degrees, rejected the value of intentionalist criticism but offered theoreticians, critics and historians of film a means
to retain director studies (albeit as author surrogates) and to value the
reader. Foucault's influence is clearly felt in Wollen's 1972 edition of *Signs
and Meaning in the Cinema*, as we saw in the previous chapter. His analysis
mirrors the auteur critic's interest in the cinematic output of the auteur but

avoids the auteur critic's Romantic conception of authorship by focusing on texts rather than intention. Stephen Heath, in his essay 'Comment on "The Idea of Authorship"', generally endorses Wollen's analysis, maintaining that the disappearance of the author of a fiction clears space for the return of the author *as fiction* (see 1981: 220). Heath bases his analysis on what is frequently referred to as the theory of the subject.[11] Geoffrey Nowell-Smith insists that this notion of the 'fiction of the author', *pace* Heath, *requires* us to consider the author of the fiction:

> It seems to me rather that the 'fiction' of the author enables us to locate an *author of the fiction* who is by no means dispersed but who in 'his' notional coherence provides the means for us to grasp the text in the moment of its production before us. (1981: 223; emphasis in original)

He endorses the separation of, for instance, John Ford from 'John Ford', noting that the latter is private to the reader and necessarily partial. Being private, the author in inverted commas cannot be then restated as a subcode of a film or collection of films. Moreover, the type of fiction films that people like Wollen and Heath have in mind are also commodities, a fact that has a substantial role to play in the circulation and appeal of film texts as authored discourses and ideological products (see Nowell-Smith 1981: 222–4). It may be sensible to distinguish the author of the fiction and the fiction of the author, but this in no way justifies abandoning the author of the fiction, since fictional authors do not produce the fictions that give them life.

Within the last thirty years or so Booth's arguments have proved productive in studies of film authorship and narration, notably in the writings of Seymour Chatman, George Wilson and Gregory Currie. Unlike Foucault's author function, Chatman's (and Booth's) implied author is a function of an individual text, not discursive systems.[12] Chatman maintains the importance of the author as the source of a fiction, but recognises that this source is separated from the text when it is released into the public sphere. We cannot attribute the attitudes and opinions conveyed in a text to its author. The reader *reconstructs* the text through engagement with it. Chatman opts for the term 'reconstructs' rather than 'constructs' to indicate clearly what he feels are two of the most self-evident, yet strangely ignored principles of a text: a text pre-exists the act of reading and was produced purposefully. In one sense, though, 'reconstruct' is a misleading term, since there is no direct correspondence between the intentions that the reader attaches to the implied author and the intentions held by the author when producing the work. Rather than a relationship of absolute fidelity, we should instead speak of approximation. There is an intent that can be read and recovered from the text without the need to resort to biography because 'the principles of invention and intent *remain* in the text' (Chatman 1990: 75; emphasis in original). Following Beardsley, Chatman points out that the voice within a text cannot be identified with that of the author without explicit evidence that connects the author and implied author (see Chatman 1978: 147). Instead, the purpose of the implied author is to embody textual attitudes. As we have seen above, the implied author enables a structural layer in fiction that allows complicated relationships between the author, the narrator and characters. The implied author will control the entire semantic and aesthetic framework of a fiction, while the narrator's voice will be restricted. The implied author enables the narrator to speak within the fiction. 'He [the implied author], or better, *it* has no voice, no direct means of communicating. It instructs us silently, through the design of the whole, with all the voices, by all the means it has chosen to let us learn' (1978: 148; emphasis in original). Chatman offers the following diagram that helps to explain the system of narrative communication in a fictional text (see 1978: 151).

By casting the implied author as the agent behind the total coherency of the fiction, Chatman provides a means for sidestepping the problem of collective authorship. Because the implied author is the *coherent voice* of a text, the complex production of the film is masked. The actual process of production is not irrelevant, but from the reader's or spectator's perspective it is not a concern for interpreting and understanding a text. Chatman follows Booth's structure closely, but disagrees on the nature of the overall coherency. For Booth it is mainly a question of the author's morality, whereas Chatman sees coherency as a fundamentally aesthetic concern (see 1978: 149). In a collaborative medium like film there is a further benefit to Chatman's configuration of the implied author. Any authorial intention, held by the screenwriter, director or producer, can easily be overcome by the multiple interventions in the production of a film. Finding a single authorial meaning, whether that of an individual or a collective, will prove troublesome.[13] Yet despite this, the majority of films still have a coherent structure and the *impression* of a single authorial perspective. The notion of the implied author in film accounts for the film's coherency but makes no demands on the production team to have developed, by camaraderie or coercion, a single intention.

Gregory Currie develops Chatman's line of argumentation, which he terms 'Implied Author Intentionalism' (1995: 245). He contrasts this with 'Real Author Intention' arguing that authorial intention may not always correspond with the meaning of a text, for reasons such as authorial error and unconscious meaning. For whatever reason, readers will invariably interpret meanings into works that were never intended by the author. This is not an error on the part of the reader, since the evidence beyond the text to guide interpretation is typically absent. To privilege and seek the real author's intentions is to risk abandoning the act of interpretation for a psychological diagnostic procedure of the biographical author. Currie does not, though, view this as a reason to abandon the notion of intention. Narrative and communicative acts require the concept of an intending agent. 'All interpretation is intentionalistic; the issue is whether we should concern ourselves with the real intentions behind the work, or the intentions which seem to have been productive of the work' (1995: 248–9). Currie maintains that Wimsatt and Beardsley's 'intentional fallacy' is generally accurate, but that this does not license the abandonment of intention. The principle of intention is essential for interpretation, even though knowledge of such intention is unattainable. The implied author fulfils this need of interpretation without requiring the validation of actual authorial intention (see 1995: 245–9).[14]

Currie recognises that a theory of implied authorship in literature cannot be applied to film without careful consideration of the fundamental differences between the representational natures of each medium. The notion of the implied author in film faces a substantial objection. With literature we have an experience of being told something. With film, however, we *see* the events of the narrative directly. Currie addresses this distinction between literature and film by first pointing out that the experiences of viewing a film and reality differ substantially. Apart from the fact that fictional characters do not exist, so we cannot see them, only the actors who portray them, the formal construction of a film produces viewing experiences impossible in the real world. Engaging a film does not entail a spectator to imagine that he or she views the action from the position of the camera – this would necessitate the spectator also to imagine that he or she jumps in space and time with every cut. In his essay 'Photography, Painting and Perception', Currie maintains that although there is a natural dependency, or counterfactual dependence, between an object and a photograph (that is, a photographic image is an index), photographically-based images (digital or analogue) are still representations. They lack the 'egocentric' information about the

> spatial and temporal relations between the object seen and ourselves ... That seeing provides us with egocentric information in [*sic*] connected to the fact that seeing is perspectival. I could not place myself in the world if I saw the world from no particular perspective. And from what perspective I see things depends on the location of my body or at least of my eyes relative to the things I see. (1991: 26)

When viewing a film the egocentric information encompasses the theatre or other viewing environment, but excludes the wider represented space of the film. With this in mind, Currie maintains that when spectating we do not see the characters or imagine we see the characters, but imagine the fiction to be the way it is represented. We imagine Sherlock Holmes to be a pipe smoker in the Holmes stories because that is part of the description we have of him. We imagine Holmes to be a pipe smoker in the Holmes films because we see Basil Rathbone smoke a pipe. Currie thus concludes 'there is no ... objection to the idea that cinematic fictions are experienced as mediated; in fact we are then *obliged* to think of them that way' (1995: 248; emphasis in original). It is the very nature of this obligation, Currie maintains, that necessitates the implied author.

George Wilson offers an interesting variation on the notion of the implied author. In *Narration in Light* he opts for the term 'implied film maker'. This is not a trivial terminological shift, but a reconception of the notion of implied authorship to account for film. Wilson justifies the notion of implied filmmakers pretty much on the same grounds that Currie justifies implied authors. His purpose is slightly different, though. He aims to explain the nature of spectatorial access to a film narrative. To do so he focuses on three narrative concerns: the distance a narrative film places a spectator from her or his normal 'habits of perception and common-sense beliefs' ('*epistemic distance*'); the

Basil Rathbone as the pipe-smoking Sherlock Holmes

quality of information that a film presents to its audience to permit, and at times misdirect, interpretation ('*epistemic reliability*'); and the amount of information conveyed through the narrative in contrast to that held by any of the characters ('*epistemic authority*') (1986: 4–5). In most films audiences are presented with more information than the characters, although some films, such as the Sherlock Holmes adaptations, tend to invert this relationship. My interest here is not in Wilson's epistemic categories, but his analysis of authorship that underscores these categories. Each element articulates an aspect through which spectators can form judgements about a film's characters and narrative as a whole. Three entities are potentially present to structure this spectatorial access: the filmmaker, the narrator and the implied filmmaker. Wilson argues that the filmmaker cannot be the central figure for roughly the same reasons that Currie offers. He rejects the narrator also, insisting upon a clear distinction between film and literature. Whereas Chatman aims to develop a structural similarity between narrators in literature and narrators in film, Wilson contests this approach, insisting that film does not portray a narrator within the fiction in the manner that literature does. If a film misleads its audience, it does so directly.[15] The perception that one has of a film is not analogous to the linguistic account of a narrator. Film addresses the eyes and ears in the same way that the real world does. Literature shows signs of an intervening agent, the entity that wrote everything down, while film does not.[16] Like Chatman, Wilson proposes that films have implied filmmakers resident outside the narrative but who direct our attention. This is literally, of course, the function of the film production team, but the concept of the implied filmmaker alleviates the problem of attributing and verifying authorial intention to a real individual and (although Wilson does not mention this) the thorny problem of explaining intention in a collective film production. Wilson's implied filmmaker is 'located wholly outside the fictional world of the narrative occurrences and yet ... perceives these occurrences as they take place' (1986: 133). It can be characterised as an ideal observer that points out the relevant story events and perspectives from which to view them, but does not get between the spectator and the events of the story. Wilson preserves the notion that when a spectator watches a film he or she becomes a directed observer of a fictional world. At the same time, his notion of the implied filmmaker provides a critical distance between the narration of a story and the story told. A spectator's sympathies and opinions are only weakly relativistic, prompted, encouraged and delimited by the implied filmmaker.

Although ranging from diverse intellectual heritages, the author surrogate arguments all suffer from the same problem. They resolve the difficulties posed by empirical authors by not discussing them. Author functions, implied authors and implied filmmakers may be useful tools for interpreting a film or a director's cinematic output, but they are silent on authors themselves. Theorists endorsing these views rightly point out that the flesh-and-blood human(s) that produced a film or work of literature is logically distinct from the entity that appears as a chimera in a text during the acts of reading and spectating. Authors produce works, readers produce author surrogates through their engagements with works. Subsequently, author surrogates are unique to each and every reader and spectator. There are as many author surrogates for a narrative as there are people that engage the fiction. The author surrogate is itself an interpretation, and cannot therefore be responsible for or prompt that interpretation. Author surrogate theories are circular. Placing the name of the director in inverted commas does not really help either. It does not allow us to understand why someone conceived two characters like Scar and Ethan in *The Searchers* (1956). To understand *The Searchers*, one must contemplate possible reasons behind this invention. Grappling with intention, as Currie recognises, is essential for interpretation. The problem is author surrogates are not *really* capable of intention.

With the exception of Barthes, the theorists discussed in this chapter are right in advocating that the pull to search for an author at the core of a work is compelling. They fail, however, to take seriously the reason for this: that films are intentionally produced human artefacts. We look for authors because there are authors, and we work to understand why they construct the works they do. Any theory of authorship that does not establish this as a central premise dodges the central question of authorship. The consequence of author surrogate theories is they construct a barrier between authorship and meaning. Authorship, as I will discuss in the final chapter, is historically rooted. Examining this root does not imply psychobiography, although Currie is correct that often criticism is nothing other than psychobiography (1995: 246). This is more a problem of poor criticism than authorship. The drive to find an author at the core of a work is not simply to attach a name or identify a genius, but to search out an interlocutor to validate a film as meaningful, and not simply a collection of markings on celluloid. To understand the author's (or authors') purpose, we should also understand the context. *The Searchers* may be able to be read as an allegory of the Korean War, but not the Vietnam War. Granted, the film may even resonate with twenty-first-century events and audiences, but these are in excess of what the film means. It is not clear how an author surrogate theory guards against extending interpretation beyond a work's intended meaning.[17] I suspect that this is not a concern for author surrogate theorists, but certainly the moment we leave intention, we leave the domain of authorship.

3   NARRATOR AND AUTHOR

One of the main challenges for film criticism and for theorising film authorship is unravelling the various 'voices' present in a film, such as those of
characters, narrators, implied authors and authors.[1] This is not simply a
problem of dialogue or narration, but of film aesthetics in general. A colour
scheme, for instance, may have as much or more to say about authorial
intent than all the dialogue in a film. Film critics typically and automatically
cast the director as the author of a film, often with the further accolade of
an auteur. This is a questionable critical approach that I seek to challenge in
this book, mainly because of the collective nature of film production as an
act of communication. The purpose of this chapter is to distinguish between
the various 'voices' in a narrative film, clearly delineating how a film can
be constructed to both express meaning and tell a story.[2] In the last chapter I will provide a theoretical justification for this reconceptualisation of
authorship; in this chapter I use the term 'authorship' only as a structured
position, or placeholder, in textual production. The identity of the author or
authors of any text is an empirical concern related to expression. In literature this is typically a straightforward concern, since the process of writing is
often solitary.[3] To simply equate a director with a writer and call the director
the author of a film avoids understanding what part of writing constitutes
authoring, and therefore what aspects of film production are authorial acts.
In this chapter I discuss the notion of 'authorship' as a category to distinguish it from narration, but make no presumptions about how the various

production roles in film relate to authorship. When I mention a director, it is because I accept that there is good reason to believe that he or she likely performed some authorial act to produce the film under consideration, but not that he or she is the sole author of the film.[4] By re-evaluating authorship in light of a theory of communication, rather than a theory of textuality, I demonstrate that authorship and narration can be delineated along the lines of expression and storytelling respectively, and that narrators and the stories they tell are authored fictions that serve expression.

This distinction between authorship and narration is premised on a fundamental principle in the nature of fiction.[5] Basically, fictions exist, the characters and events of fictions do not. Sir Arthur Conan Doyle wrote the Sherlock Holmes stories, and I can hold a copy of a collection of his stories in my hand. The character Sherlock Holmes never existed. Although Holmes is allegedly based on Dr Joseph Bell, a lecturer at the University of Edinburgh, Holmes and Bell are not, nor could they be, the same. The statement 'Sherlock Holmes is a detective' is false, not because Holmes did another job, but because the Sherlock Holmes of the stories has never existed for anything to be true of him. However, the stories exist, and in these stories Holmes is a detective, so the statement 'in the Sherlock Holmes stories, Sherlock Holmes is a detective' is true. Similarly, Watson can call Holmes his friend because it is true in the stories that they are friends, but I cannot state truthfully that Watson and Holmes are friends without qualifying 'within the Sherlock Holmes stories' for the same reason I cannot state truthfully, without qualification, that Holmes is a detective.[6] It is this distinction between the story world and the world of texts and readers that delimits the spheres of narrators and authors respectively, regardless of the medium. Narrators tell the story of the fiction; authors construct the fiction, its narrator(s), characters and events to entertain and to communicate allegorically.

Wayne Booth's arguments about literary narration have significantly influenced theories of narration in film. It will be useful to begin a discussion of film narrators and authors by examining these views. Booth argues that readers experience both a narrator (or narrators) who tells the story and an idealised impression of the author, or 'implied author', that can be construed as conveying the complex network of meanings and impressions a reader interprets from a work. The narrator and implied author differ, in that the 'narrator' is usually taken to mean the 'I' of a work, but the 'I' is seldom if ever identical with the implied image of the artist ... Our sense of the implied author includes not only the extractable meanings but also the moral and emotional content of each bit of action and suffering of all the characters. It includes, in short, the intuitive apprehension of a completed artistic whole; the chief value to which *this* implied author is committed, regardless of what party his creator belongs to in real life. (1991: 73-4; emphasis in original).

My concern is to separate narrators from authors and implied authors, so I will not go into extensive detail about the numerous permutations of narrators that Booth elaborates in his book. The term 'narrator' really stands for a class of fictional entities that can convey a story. For instance, in the novel *Double Indemnity* (1936) James M. Cain constructs a story told through the written account of its main character, Walter Huff. Huff is an example of what Booth calls a 'dramatised narrator'. Booth identifies two types of dramatised narrators: 'observers' and 'narrator-agents'. Both types are part of the story, but the former reports on events in the fiction while the latter plays a significant role in these events. Huff is a narrator-agent. A narrator who asserts her or his presence (usually through the utterance of 'I' or 'we') but maintains a distance from the drama Booth calls an 'undramatised narrator'. Such narration will typically be somewhat impersonal. In novels where there is no explicit reference to an implied author the undramatised narrator and implied author will be one and the same narrating agent, since the narration is experienced as if the author is narrating the story (see Booth 1991: 149–54). Booth's implied authors are principal narrators that relegate and rescind narrative control to other story and character narrators. A significant aspect of interpretation involves evaluating agreements and disagreements between narrating voices.

The film *Double Indemnity* (1944) also has a dramatised narrator-agent in the character Walter Neff (Huff's name in the film). His voiceover narration is narrativised as a confession being recorded on a Dictaphone, thereby structuring the film as a recollection.[7] Despite this, we still see events unfold as if we are taken back in time to witness the crimes. We seem to experience each scene directly rather than through a narrator. David Bordwell takes this direct spectatorial experience seriously as a general principle in narrative film and argues against narrators and implied authors. Where there is no experience of a narrator, he insists, there is no justification for imposing one. Whatever value narrators have for literature they are an 'anthropomorphic fiction' in film employed only to satisfy the requirements of a theory of narration rooted in a theory of communication. Bordwell instead proposes a more parsimonious, constructivist model. Spectators, he contends, construct film narratives from the audio-visual cues in the text. 'This presupposes a perceiver, but not a sender, of a message' (1985: 62). In the odd

Walter Neff (Fred MacMurray) tells the story of his crimes in *Double Indemnity* (1944)

instances where a narrative voice is perceived in a film, it appears as the consequence of reading a film and not the source of narration (see 1985: 61–2). In *Making Meaning* Bordwell elaborates on these views. Critics may construct an impression of a filmmaker or narrator to aid interpretation, an interpretative practice Bordwell calls 'personification', but this does not justify asserting that a personified filmmaker or narrator actually tells a film (see 1989: 151–68).[8]

Bordwell offers a sober analysis, but it is ultimately too reductive. He is correct that narrators do not create narrations. From the perspective of causation we can eliminate all entities apart from real authors communicating with real spectators. The problem is what we might call his 'flat pack' approach: 'narration is better understood as the organisation of a set of cues for the construction of a story' (1985: 62). Film seems to be much more than a set of audio-visual cues and a schematic in the form of a narrative that allows a spectator to construct a story, especially as the narrative itself needs first to be interpreted. Films are projected already assembled. Granted, inference is required to comprehend a film, but this does not justify constructivism any more than an answer to the question 'could you pass the salt?' does. Inference is aimed at intention. If I simply answer this question 'yes, I could' and keep eating, I have probably not inferred my companion's intention correctly. If instead I pass the salt, I likely have. My dinner companion, I suspect, is not interested in my salt-moving capacities as such, except that they are employed in helping her to season her food. The converse could be true if my dinner companion was a medical doctor and I was complaining of limited arm movement. Either response could be correct, but to respond to the question appropriately I need to be able to assess her intention for asking it. This will require me to evaluate the question in the context of, for instance, the setting and the conversation we are having. Inference in film spectation is no different. To understand a film is to understand why it was constructed in the way that it was. Composing a meaning is different from understanding one. Just as I can infer at least two meanings from 'could you pass the salt?', a film spectator can infer, and therefore construct, all sorts of fictions and narrations from the audio-visual data on screen and a dollop of reason to connect them. My disagreement with Bordwell is not with his reliance on inference – I think he is basically correct on this point – but his abandonment of intention to direct inference. Instead, he argues that filmmakers 'aim to make certain sorts of objects, which in turn produce more or less predictable effects when used in conventional ways' (1989: 268). Convention is important, but is not by itself sufficient for interpretation. Such a focus on convention leads us to interpret through the most likely conventional usage, rather than to assess what was actually meant. In most instances 'could you pass the salt?' means 'pass the salt', but not all. Without attention to the agent's intent we have limited means to choose between comparable interpretations, or recognise alternative purposes behind seemingly conventional representations.

Bordwell further objects to film narrators on the grounds that if films had narrators, spectators should experience a film through an 'invisible observer's' perspective. However, the plasticity of film form typically presents a visual perspective on narrative events that are impossible. Editing, odd framings, black-and-white images, manipulations of colour, temporal and spatial discontinuity, and so on, do not correspond with normal ways of seeing. An 'invisible observer' approach to filmmaking is possible, but only as a contingent, stylistic choice. I agree with Bordwell that 'invisible observer' theories of film narration should be abandoned, but dispute that this implies that film spectators have no experience of being told a story. The formal and aesthetic choices made by filmmakers, the use or avoidance of genre, the selection of actors and stars, and the creation of special effects are all organised to allow comprehension of both a story and the reason for telling it. By constructing films so they can be understood as individual, coherent tales, filmmakers construct narrators into their films. Bordwell's mistake is to assume that a narrator theory implies that a film's optical perspective is also its narrative perspective.

Tom Gunning broadly accepts Bordwell's constructivist argument, but also questions his elision of film narrators. Through his historical and critical investigations into silent film, Gunning establishes a distinction between showing and telling in film. Novels tell stories, he maintains, films primarily show them. Photographic representations are complex, though, and identifying what is narratively significant from what is not requires guidance. 'The primary task of the filmic narrator must be to overcome the initial resistance of the photographic material to telling by creating a hierarchy of narratively important elements within a mass of contingent detail' (1991: 17). Gunning theorises this proposal through Stephen Heath's concept of 'narrativisation'. For Gunning, this term names the process of directing the spectator's attention to significant aspects of the images, thereby enabling interpretation, and effectively transforming the showing of images to the telling of a story via these images (see 1991:17–8). One of the main challenges we face when examining and distinguishing between film authorship and narration is overcoming our familiarity with classical film construction. For this reason, Gunning's focus on narration in D. W. Griffith's early films is invaluable. It is much easier to see the relationship between authorship and narration when analysing less familiar forms of filmmaking. I will demonstrate the shift from showing to telling that Gunning describes, and the relationship between narrative and authorial voices, through the 1914 Italian film *Cabiria*, directed by Giovanni Pastrone.

One of the many reasons for *Cabiria*'s popularity and its significance in film history is its slow, smooth and methodical camera movements, now known as 'Cabiria movement'. These camera movements are more than stylistic embellishments to the film, they function narratively and semantically. The film is set during the Punic Wars. Fulvius Axilla, a Roman patrician and spy, and his slave Maciste, are working covertly in Carthage when they accept the task of rescuing a little girl, Cabiria, from being sacrificed to the God Moloch. Fulvius and Maciste succeed, and are subsequently pursued by Moloch's worshipers. They take refuge in an attic room at the Striped Monkey, a local inn run by the shifty Bodastoret. This scene, constituted by a single tracking shot, is clearly shot on a set. Strangely, a pillar has been placed on set in such a manner that it occupies the centre of

Cabiria (1914): Fulvius (Umberto Mozzato), Maciste (Bartolomeo Pagano) and Cabiria (Carolina Catena) take refuge in the attic at the Striped Monkey (above left); Bodastoret (Raffaele Di Napoli) enters through a hatch door (above right) on the right side of the set (bottom-centre of the frame) to bring food and news

Bodastoret, Fulvius and Maciste 'discuss' a threat to Rome (above left), then plan to save themselves and Rome (above right)

the frame, bisecting the image.[9] This pillar, in conjunction with the camera movement, is crucial for understanding the character concerns and meaning of the sequence. Action and conversation occurring to the left of the pillar involves the security of Rome, while action to the right focuses on the individual wellbeing of the characters. It is also important to keep in mind that Fulvius Axillus serves Rome, and Maciste serves Fulvius Axillus. The scene opens with Fulvius to the left of the pillar, Maciste and Cabiria to the right. Maciste mends Cabiria's clothes. Fulvius moves to the right of the pillar to look out of the window to see if they have been discovered. The camera tracks right so all we can see is the set on the right side of the pillar when Bodastoret enters bringing food. He and Fulvius move to the left side of the pillar to discuss news of a threat to Rome. The camera tracks left with them while Maciste returns to mending Cabiria's dress on the right side of the pillar. Then everyone moves to the left of the frame when it has been decided to escape Carthage to warn of the plot against Rome. The scene ends with Fulvius, Maciste and Cabiria on the left of the frame. Cabiria eats while the two men plan their escape. The staging and camera movement focuses audience attention on the shifting character interests from personal safety to the security of Rome. By ending on the left the point is clear: personal and political securities are inseparable, and indeed individual needs are subordinate to the requirements and defence of the state. This view reflects more than just patriotism, but a strong nationalist and imperialist perspective in Italy in the 1910s that rooted itself, both culturally and politically, in the ancient Roman Empire and motivated exploits like the invasion of Libya.[10]

In the palace xxx Tom ask me about ellipses

In this scene the camera follows the action. In the next scene it leads it. The scene begins with the requisite 'Diva' shot. Sophonisba, daughter of Hasdrubal, strokes her pet leopard, then stares seductively into the camera, her bust heaving. An intertitle follows, stating that Hasdrubal promises his beautiful daughter to his guest, the Numidian king Massinissa. The next shot is a long take of a large room in the palace. The camera inexplicably begins to track diagonally towards the stairs. As the camera moves into the scene, completely disrupting the proscenium-like framing that begins the

The camera tracks diagonally to the right

shot, Massinissa enters and picks up an object sitting inconspicuously to the right of the steps. He then walks towards the camera while the camera continues to track towards the stairs. As Massinissa moves into a medium-long shot, Sophonisba's servant enters from the left of the frame. The two characters *and the camera* meet as Massinissa hands Sophonisba's gift to her servant. The camera has been tracking to this point even before the characters enter the frame. The camera is perfectly situated so we also see that this exchange is being observed. We learn from this sequence not only of

The camera movement anticipates the meeting between Massinissa (Vitale De Stefano) and Sophonisba's servant

Massinissa's interest in Sophonisba, but also that we are being told this story by someone or something that is already aware of the key events yet to occur and duly directs our attention.

Both the film's narration and its meaning are authorial concerns, but should not be conflated. The filmmakers use the camera work in these sequences, in combination with the choreography, to tell the story by focusing spectators on key events in the frame, and use these key events and their telling to make clear the film's nationalist concerns. Whether we conceive the narrator as a fictional entity or real individual(s) that constructs the story is, for the moment, immaterial. It is enough that these scenes betray the intentional act of directing spectator attention – of narrating. Where we have an intentional act, there must also be an agent performing this act. For this reason Bordwell's notion of 'a message without a sender' would constitute no message at all. Messages and stories come about through intentional human actions. Questions like 'how do I construct the story from the pillar or the camera movement?' will not get us far, but 'why did the filmmakers place the pillar in the centre of the frame and move the camera the way they did?' will. It is the act of focusing spectator attention that requires us to acknowledge the presence of a narrator. Our concern should not be whether films have narrators, but who or what these narrators might be.

There are a few contenders for this role: fictional characters within the story, fictional narrators outside of the story, implied authors (and implied filmmakers) and real authors. I will begin with implied authors and filmmakers. Wayne Booth uses the concept of implied authors to inoculate real authors against the responsibility for readers' interpretations. He begins innocently enough by asserting that if interpretation occurs in communication, then there must be a source of the meaning. From here his analysis goes awry. He reasons that since meanings may or may not correspond to the intentions or beliefs of the real author, it would be incorrect to attribute any meaning understood to that person's intentions. Instead, meaning is better attributed to a fictional counterpart – an implied author – who can safely hold the opinions attributed. I am not convinced that Booth has identified a problem to resolve, and even if he has, I am not persuaded that an implied author is up to the task. The implied author is a tautological entity. Being equivalent to a spectator's interpretation, the implied author is imposed as the source of the meaning that the spectator has already understood. As Mieke Bal states, 'the implied author is the result of the investigation of the meaning of the text and not the source of that meaning' (1997: 18). In effect, it misplaces the location of interpretation from the spectator or reader back onto the text itself and construes it as a pseudo intention. The implied author is merely a nominal addition that does not add to our understanding of texts or the process of narration. Furthermore, the implied author undermines the very communicative model on which it relies by introducing a concept or entity not part of normal communication. In conversation we often misunderstand each other. We do not introduce 'implied conversationalists' to account for these misunderstandings. One may respond that in conversation speakers can be questioned to improve comprehension, whereas filmmakers typically cannot. Like film, journalism often does not enable reply. Are we to invent 'implied journalists' when listening to or reading reports in a newspaper, on radio or on television? Unlikely. Fidelity between intention and interpretation rests with a reader's obligation to evaluate intention. Theorists endorsing the notion of implied authors often write about meaning as if it implies immediate and exact correspondence between speaker and listener. It doesn't. Understanding meaning is an imperfect process with room for error and improvement. Interpretation can also locate ideas never intended. Why attribute these to an implied author when they frequently stem from a reader's or spectator's lateral thinking? Semantic infidelity between expression and reception does not justify fictional author surrogates. We are better off talking of spectator interpretations and actual author meanings.

In practice, I am not proposing anything new. While theorists propose narratological entities like implied authors and filmmakers, practitioners of film history and criticism frequently proceed to take into account the actual author or authorial body of a film. *The Birth of a Nation* (D. W. Griffith, 1915) forwards an anti-integrationalist viewpoint that has rightly been attacked as racist, from the day the film was released to the present. Criticism and historical analysis of *The Birth of a Nation* do not attribute the film's racist perspective to 'D. W. Griffith', *the implied filmmaker*, but to D. W. Griffith, *the actual man who directed and, with Frank E. Woods, wrote the film*, and also to Thomas W. Dixon, the author of *The Clansman* – the novel and stage play on which the film is largely based.[11] This is how it should be. We are not concerned with the views of a fictional entity we construct out of our experience with a text, but the views of the actual flesh-and-blood people who are responsible for them. Individuals produce representations for reasons, and as spectators it is our duty to engage that person's (or those persons') reasons for doing so.

I have used the examples of *Cabiria* and *The Birth of a Nation* to contend that authors are accountable for meaning and that narrative films have narrators who convey stories. The question I will address now is do both these tasks require one entity, an author, or two, an author and narrator? Examining the various types of narrators available will help to answer this question. Gregory Currie notes that in literature, controlling narrators are fictionally responsible for the text, including those stories told by embedded narrators. In both literature and film embedded narrators are contingently present. Literature and film differ, he insists, in that the former possesses controlling narrators necessarily, the latter never possesses them. With literature, he explains, 'it is often natural to imagine that what one is reading is a true account of certain events witnessed or otherwise known about by someone, who then went to the trouble of setting it all down for us in writing' (1995: 266). From this he concludes that the idea of a controlling filmic narrator going through the trouble and expense of creating a film is absurd, especially for narratives whose diegesis is pre-cinematic. I agree, such a scenario would be absurd, but I do not see this as an argument against controlling narrators in film. Currie assumes that the medium a fiction is rendered in is also the medium in which a narrator renders her or his narrative. This cannot be correct, and character narrators provide evidence why this is the case. In *Rashomon* (1950), character narrators narrate the individual stories of the crime.[12] None of the stories (or at best one story) accurately relates the events, so to some degree the events we see are fictional inventions of fictional characters from a pre-cinematic age. Under Currie's analysis, character narrators can narrate non-cinematically pre-cinematic events, but no controlling narrator is capable of telling the story of the divergent stories. This seems an odd conclusion. However, even the notion that in literature a narrator sets down the story in writing is problematic. If this were correct, then there should be no stories that diegetically predate writing. Yet Jean M. Auel's *Clan of Cave Bear* (1980) is precisely such a novel. Clearly illiterate and pre-literary narrators in literary fiction are possible. It seems that narrators make no necessary commitments to media, authors do. With this restriction removed, there should be no problem entertaining the view that films have controlling narrators necessarily.

My example of *Cabiria* demonstrates that markers of a narrator are there for anyone wishing to look for them, a view Gunning defends also. Even the most seemingly transparent visual presentations, he argues, still require a source: 'the alert and active spectator proposed by Bordwell's psychological description must realise that these images come from *somewhere*' (1991: 23; emphasis in original). Strangely, Gunning's *'somewhere,'* is not a narrator-agent, but a *narrative discourse* composed of 'images and their constructions' (ibid.). Gunning's narrator is an author surrogate constructed through the act of reading to satisfy a logical requirement of a communication model of narration. This is precisely the type of argument Bordwell warns against, and with good reason. The tautology it generates, the same tautology that the implied author generates, reduces the narrator to a trivial entity and is more objectionable than the logical problem it is meant to resolve. In contrast, I propose taking Gunning's *'somewhere'* more seriously. Film images and the focus on detail within them do come from somewhere: the filmmaker(s). This may appear far too simple a suggestion to be of much theoretical value, but it seems to me that in much of our theory we have lost sight of the purposes and practices of fiction making. Fiction is a useful means for an agent (or agents) to communicate ideas about our world, from the profound to the trivial, through (often entertaining) allegories. For this reason it makes sense to me that a theory of authorship should start from the basic principles of communication and develop to account for the means of communication. In the case of narrative film this means communicating through story *and* through film.[13]

One could, from this argument, conclude that there is no point in talking about implied authors and narrators, since it is really a film's authorial team that narrates the story and develops the film in such a way that it conveys intended meaning. I agree the implied author should be set aside. We do not need a theoretical entity to account for interpretation. There is a difference between constructing a film and telling a story, though. Bordwell (1985) objects that narrators add unnecessary theoretical entities to our model of film fiction. Yet as the example of *Rashomon* demonstrates, the presence of a controlling narrator adds only one further agent to a fiction of a type already well established. A narrator is a fictional character in the fiction tasked with telling a story, and is as much an authorial construction as any other character or event in the fiction. Moreover, it is no more an imposition on the story than a historian is on the history he or she narrates. The reason for proposing the presence of controlling narrators in narrative films is not that they *could* be part of a fiction, but that they *must* be part of any fiction. They solve a logical problem. As I indicated at the start of this chapter, true statements within fictions are world-bound. The short story 'The Hound of the Baskervilles' (1901–02) exists, but not Sherlock Holmes and Dr John Watson. The statement 'Sir Arthur Conan Doyle wrote "The Hound of the Baskervilles"' is true, but not 'Sherlock Holmes discovered that Stapleton attempted to kill Sir Henry', only because Holmes, Stapleton and Sir Henry have never existed for anything to be true of them. As the narrator in the stories Doyle published in *The Strand*, Dr Watson can state truthfully that 'Sherlock Holmes discovered that Stapleton attempted to kill Sir Henry' because it is true in the world of Sherlock Holmes, of which Watson is a member. In the Basil Rathbone/Nigel Bruce film version of this story (1939), Watson does not appear to be the controlling narrator. From this we should conclude that the filmmakers constructed an anonymous controlling narrator (or undramatised narrator) typical of other classical Hollywood films, not that the film lacks a narrator. The *experience* spectators have of watching films need not govern the narrative structure of films. Cinematic images of fictions are representational, not presentational.

Citizen Kane (1941) is an ideal film to illustrate the relationships between character narrators, controlling narrators and authors that I have been developing. The film possesses two incongruities that can be resolved by close attention to the narrative and authorial voices in the film.

Citizen Kane (1941): The closed door (above left), seen through the broken globe, suggests Charles Foster Kane (Orsen Welles) died alone; the nurse, seen reflected in the broken globe (above right), enters the room after Kane has died

First, Thompson's task is to make sense of Kane's dying word, 'Rosebud', but the images presented at the beginning of the film suggest that Kane is alone in the room at the time of his death. His nurse enters only after the snow globe breaks and the word has been spoken. There are three possible explanations: (1) Welles made an error in filming; (2) the images mislead purposely; or (3) nobody knows if Kane said 'Rosebud'.[14] Second, the first Susan Alexander Kane sequence has no obvious purpose in the film. Thompson sees Susan, is rebuffed, then goes away to read Thatcher's diary. Why bother including this scene when all the information it presents (basically that Susan has taken to drink) could simply be included when Thompson interviews her later in the film? It could easily be cut without any risk to the film's story or clarity. Identifying the purpose of Thompson's first attempted interview with Susan will provide the key for explaining the 'Rosebud' dilemma – not what it means as a summation of Kane's life, but its purpose in the film. Mapping out the film's sequences aids this task.

'No Trespassing' (Camera moves up the chain link fence)

    Kane's deathbed and statement 'Rosebud'

    Newsreel and post-film discussion

        Susan Alexander Kane – failed interview

            Thatcher's story (via manuscript)
            Mr Bernstein's story
            Jedediah Leland's story

        Susan Alexander Kane's story

    Raymond's story

    Destruction of Kane's possessions, including 'Rosebud'

'No Trespassing' (Camera moves down the chain link fence)

This diagram makes clear the film's structural symmetry, something that should already be evident from the 'No Trespassing' signs that bracket the film. At the heart of the film are the three stories from the people that knew Kane from his formative years. Once we step outside of this group, the bracketing becomes evident. The first Susan Alexander Kane sequence is required to preserve this symmetry. The destruction of Kane's property completes his death.[15] This leaves Raymond's story paired with the newsreel sequence. I contend that Raymond is the source of the story about Kane's last word, which he basically admits after his interview with Thompson, and therefore the cause of Thompson's quest for 'Rosebud'. This gains further support when we see Raymond with the journalists at the Kane estate just prior to the incineration of Rosebud, thereby reinforcing the symmetry with the newsreel sequence.

Raymond being the source of the word 'Rosebud' is not contentious. He admits to Thompson:

> yea, I heard him say it that other time too. He just said ... 'Rosebud', then he dropped the glass ball and it broke on the floor. He didn't say anything after that and I knew he was dead. He said all kinds of things that didn't mean anything.

Rather, the question is whether Raymond reports or invents the details of Kane's death. Raymond's account corresponds with the way we see Kane die, but contradicts on the issue of Raymond's presence. This is not the only reason for us to question the veracity of Kane's death scene. Although, as André Bazin (1991) rightly notes, the film is known for its realist, deep focus cinematography, Kane's death scene is remarkably stylised. The sequence begins with a long shot of Kane lying in bed. This realist image is interrupted by a superimposition of snow onto the frame. Behind the

Citizen Kane (1941): A non-realist, superimposed shot depicts one of Kane's final moments

snow is a dissolve from Kane to a miniature snow-covered house. The camera pulls back to show that the miniature is in a snow globe. The snow globe is not the source of the snow in the frame, though. The superimposed snow continues until the snow globe breaks, marking Kane's death. Just prior to Kane's death we are provided with a close-up of Kane whispering 'Rosebud', and hear the word saturated in reverb. This is followed by an image of the globe falling from Kane's hand. The framing then shifts almost 180 degrees as we see the globe in close-up hit the floor. A distorted image of the nurse entering the room follows, shot through the broken globe. The sound of the globe breaking is presented in the non-diegetic music, not as a diegetic sound. We return to the previous framing to see Kane at the top of the image and a reflection in the broken globe of the nurse walking towards him. The scene then returns to a realist aesthetic, with the nurse folding Kane's arms and covering him with a sheet. The final shot repeats the initial framing of the sequence, bracketing it. At no point is Raymond's presence in the room even hinted at, even though the styl-ised images correspond with the story Raymond tells Thompson.

Citizen Kane (1941): Superimpositions persist until Kane's death

Of the possible explanations for this anomaly in the film, the strongest seems to me to be that Raymond was not in the room and he invented the story of Kane's last word.[16] Raymond is not necessarily wrong about Kane's last word, but like Kane he hypothesises from available, but inconclusive evidence. Raymond witnesses Kane smashing up Susan's room. The last shot of the sequence places the camera near a snow globe. As Kane picks this up, his rage dies down. Standing at the door to the room, with the staff looking on, Kane says 'Rosebud', and then walks out of the room. When the same globe is seen smashed on the floor following Kane's death, there is good reason to assume 'Rosebud' could have been on his mind. Raymond's trick was to extrapolate this limited evidence into a plausible and interest-ing story. It is far more poetic if the word signals Kane's last thought rather than the end of his marriage. We see Kane do something similar when he instructs that a reporter be sent to Brooklyn to confront a husband about his missing wife and accuse him of murder. Kane is acting opportunistically based on insufficient information, and on the very same night that he pens his 'Declaration of Principles'. Both Raymond's Rosebud story and Kane's murder story *may* be true in the fiction, neither is proved nor disproved, but this is not the point. Rather, it is the public interest these stories generate that is significant. Kane states 'if the headline is big enough, it makes the news big enough'. Raymond learned this lesson also. 'Rosebud' is certainly a big headline that changes the mere passing of a man into an enigma about his existence. Raymond's motivation seems financial. He is self-serving, but not a criminal. In reply to Thompson's question about 'Rosebud', Raymond states: 'Rosebud? I'll tell you about Rosebud. How much is it worth to you? $1000?' This is certainly not an excessive amount of money, especially when contrasted with what he could obtain by lifting a few choice items from the estate. By initiating the 'Rosebud' story, Raymond tries to place himself as *the* source of information within the Kane house, a position that could pay well over time, or perhaps in some other way affect his social status. His motives, however, remain somewhat mysterious. Raymond fails to earn his price because the story he tells fails to live up to the myth he caused. Thompson explains: 'I don't think any word can explain a man's life.' After being rebuffed by Thompson, Raymond turns his attention to the value of the Kane estate. Perhaps the great irony of the film is that it is Raymond who instructs the sled to be thrown on the fire, unaware of the word 'Rosebud' painted on it. It seems to me hard to make sense of the inconsistency between the images of Kane's death, which depict him alone in the room, and Raymond's story of Kane's death, which implies Raymond's presence, without recognising that we were presented with a perspective on Raymond that signals this discrepancy. Examining the film's narrative strategy reveals how much it relies on 'telling' over the evidence of showing. One message of the film is telling rarely, if ever, is uncoupled from the interests of the teller.

Previously I stated that a film's author(s) construct its narrative and narrator(s). By 'author' I do not simply mean the director, although the director will often be among the most significant members of the production team. I am referring instead to what will typically be a collection of people responsible for structuring a film so that it has the properties and meanings that it does. I will have more to say about the theory of a collective authorship in the final chapter. My point here is that the narrative structures, formal construction, the script, the acting, the music, sound, lighting, cinematography, sets, and so on, are worked into the film, for the most part, purposefully. However, to be a member of a production team does not imply one is also a member of its authorial collective. Authorship is not about being able to use a camera, write a script, act a prescribed role or even direct actors to behave a certain way. In short, authorship is not equatable to production roles, although certain production roles, like director and screenwriter, lend themselves to authorial contributions better than, for instance, dialogue editor and focus puller. The question of authorship targets the people who conceive, develop and realise the coherent narrative, aesthetic and thematic unity of a film. For example, Robert L. Carringer (1996), in his exhaustive research into the production history of *Citizen Kane*, demonstrates the extent to which the film was a collaborative production, arguing that Welles' acclaim as the sole author of the film was always more a consequence of his self-publicity and auteur criticism than a rigorous consideration of the actual manner through which the film came into being. Any analysis of the film's authorship that does not consider, for a start, the contributions of at least Herman Mankiewicz, who co-wrote the screenplay with Welles, cinematographer Gregg Toland and composer Bernard Herrmann, cannot accurately account for the film's aesthetics and themes.[17]

Once we begin to accept the contributions of other members of the production team, we can no longer retain the subject-centred reason on which auteur criticism relies. Film production involves communication and negotiation between members of the production team and will, by virtue of the knowledge each brings to the process, engage a wide range of ideas, perspectives and filmmaking practices. Moreover, filmmaking is a cultural practice that engages with the world and communicates views back to an audience – views that can range from those deeply considered to the utterly trivial. As a result, we should expect to be able to recognise clear lineages through and intertextual relationships between film texts, including the full range of semantic and aesthetic concerns. This does not require us to presume that every intertextual relationship a critic may find implies that a writer, director, producer, cinematographer, and so on, had that specific film or novel in mind, any more than we should presume that a writer is aware of the full etymological history of any word he or she uses. Nor does it imply that a broader film culture speaks through filmmakers. Historical and cultural representational conventions do not justify sliding down the slippery slope to the death of the author or author surrogates. Rather, it means that there are complex and historically variable cultural contexts and conventions that authors communicate through intentionally. The readability of a work depends upon the competency of the author(s) to use the medium and its conventions to express ideas.[18] Likewise, the quality of an interpretation depends on the reader's or spectator's relevant knowledge. In practice, an author's meanings and reader's or spectator's interpretations will not fully correspond. This does not license us to abandon intention for interpretation, but challenges us to better refine our critical analyses.

There are two principal reasons for gaps between an author's intention and a reader's interpretation: misreadings and 'unintended meanings'. Misreading will typically relate to a failure to express or understand intention due to the author's or reader's limited competency with the medium.[19] 'Unintended meanings' instead identify additions to the intended meaning. Again, no theoretical author surrogates or appeal to the unfathomable depths of an author's psyche are required. 'Unintended meanings' can be accounted for through a straightforward intersubjective process we encounter every day: communication.[20] Jürgen Habermas explains why. 'The lifeworld forms a horizon and at the same time offers a store of things taken for granted in the given culture from which communicative participants draw consensual interpretative patterns in their efforts at interpretation' (1987: 298). Communication is not the process of a reader reaching into a speaker's mind, but of a speaker expressing outwards, performing communicative acts through available and shared cultural forms. It presumes a recipient sufficiently versed in the relevant cultural forms to understand the meaning intended, although not necessarily with absolute fidelity.

I have put the term 'unintended meanings' in inverted commas because although it is commonly used and understood, I wish instead to use E. D. Hisrch's term 'significance', which seems to better evoke the socio-cultural lifeworld foundation of intersubjective reason. Understanding a work, Hirsch argues, constitutes understanding its meaning and significance. Meaning corresponds with an author's intention; significance relates the text outwards towards a broader set of relations. In practice the analysis of both meaning and significance are interrelated, and the boundary can be difficult to define. Practical difficulties, though, need not curtail theoretical classification:

> By 'understanding', therefore, I mean a perception or construction of the author's verbal meaning, nothing more, nothing less. The significance of that meaning, its relation to ourselves, to history, to the author's personality, even to the author's other works can be something objective and is frequently even more important. What shall we call that function by which we perceive significance?

The obvious choice is 'judgement': one understands meaning;
one judges significance. (Hirsch 1967: 143)

Hirsch places a great deal of emphasis on significance, and with good
reason. A principal objective of the act of criticism is to evaluate the
manner in which the meaning of a work resonates with broader socio-cultural concerns. Even the most erudite meaning can lack value if it does not
engage a public context. By 'public context' I am not referring to explicit
intertextual references that inform part of the film's meaning. These are
rooted in intention. Rather, I am concerned with critical judgements that
position the work and its authorship within socio-cultural discourses, in
light of the meaning. The *Manchurian Candidate* (1962), directed by John
Frankenheimer, is a useful film to illustrate the difference between understanding meaning and judging significance.

Griel Marcus asserts that the success of the film depends not just on
the quality of the script, but a devoted cast and crew 'diving into material
they've chosen, or been given, and in every case outstripping the material and themselves' (2002: 34). The film is a direct attack on the House
Un-American Activities Committee (HUAC) and Senator Joseph McCarthy.
It avoids engaging in the polemics of American democracy and Soviet
Communism prevalent at the time and that underscored the 'healthy' culture of 'red-baiting' films of the period. Instead, the film opts for a different
path, asserting the absolute value and right of the inalienable principles
of American democracy against challenges to it, both internal and external.
The film depicts precisely how un-American a body like HUAC, tasked with
enforcing 'American democracy', was, and indeed how much it mirrored
the very totalitarian state and principles it despised.[21] In *The Manchurian
Candidate* the threats to American society come from the Soviet agents
that infiltrate the United States and its military, but most significantly their
allegiance with fascists within the American government and the willing-
ness of these individuals to abandon democratic principles for political
power and personal gain. This is not the first film that located threats to the
ideal of American democracy within the very practice of American democracy. This is also common to some of the films directed by Frank Capra.[22]

The Manchurian Candidate does not appear to directly and intentionally
reference Capra's films, but echoes some of their aesthetics and themes.
The list of films directed by Capra that I will discuss is conservative. I will

consider his more overtly ideological films that, as Robert Sklar and Vito Zagarrio point out, have received the most scholarly attention: *Mr. Deeds Goes to Town* (1936), *Mr. Smith Goes to Washington* (1939), *Meet John Doe* (1941) and *It's a Wonderful Life* (1946) (Sklar & Zagarrio 1998: 3).[23] Sklar notes that Capra did not criticise 'the American social and economic system, did not even want a redistribution of wealth and power. He simply wanted more neighbourly and responsible people at the top of the social and economic hierarchy' (1994: 210). Sklar is also correct that these films do not pit small-town and big-city America against each other, although clearly the provincial environments typically epitomise a neighbourliness that needs to be learned in the city. The leading male characters in these films, Longfellow Deeds, Jefferson Smith, John Doe/Long John Willoughby and George Bailey, are all small-town boys. The first three are pilloried in the city press because of their 'yokelness'. Deeds and Smith suffer most from the press and would just as quickly assist those in need as punch those who provoke. Despite (or perhaps because of) their odd but just burst of violence, their simplicity and good nature overcomes the cynicism of Babe Bennett (*Mr. Deeds Goes to Town*) and Clarissa Saunders (*Mr. Smith Goes to Washington*). This small-town neighbourliness also appears in *The Manchurian Candidate*, through the hospitality shown by Jocelyn and her father, Senator Thomas Jordan, out at the lake. The countryside is not wholly idyllic, though: corruption and selfishness has invaded, as Raymond's mother and her second husband, Senator John Iselin, take up residence in the country home Raymond's biological father bequeathed to Raymond. Not that corruption and selfishness remain distant from Capra's small towns: Taylor's men invade to break up the Boy Ranger press in *Mr. Smith Goes to Washington* and Bedford Falls has the luck to have Henry F. Potter as a resident in *It's a Wonderful Life*.

Capra does more than avoid criticising American economic, social and political life, he absolutely endorses them, suggesting that the selfish and the corrupt, the John Cedars (*Mr. Deeds Goes to Town*), Jim Taylors (*Mr. Smith Goes to Washington*), D. B. Nortons (*Meet John Doe*) and the Mr Potters (*It's a Wonderful Life*) can all be defeated by community actions.[24] The worlds of Capra's films remain fundamentally sound and humane, and community spirit is sufficient to put right the acts of selfish individuals. These films are very much of the late Depression and early postwar years where this optimism was more or less warranted. *The Manchurian*

Candidate is of a different time with different problems. The threats are no longer just about having a roof and food, as serious as these problems were, but of nuclear annihilation and control over one's own mental capacities. It is a world where the Jefferson Smiths and John Does have not been able to defeat the Jim Taylors and D. B. Nortons, who have gained power. Capra's communities seem to have migrated to become the urban masses at political rallies. It is a society so drenched in fear that a charge of communism, regardless of whether it is accurate, is sufficient to condemn. More troubling is the bald lie that this charge has, as the person making it, Raymond's mother, colludes with communist states to take the White House undemocratically through deceit and murder. Capra's villains take advantage of America's political and economic systems, whereas the Iselins assault it. *The Manchurian Candidate* presents a world where Capra's neighbourliness has more or less failed, leaving Raymond alone to defend basic human and democratic principles, not with words, but with a sniper's riffle. The film, like Capra's films, offers no challenge to American democratic principles, but depicts the extensive damage to these principles done by restricting self-determination and free speech through something as un-American as McCarthy's House Un-American Activities Committee.

There are other similarities between these films, but there is no need to labour this analysis here. It would be a mistake, as far as I can tell, to suggest that *The Manchurian Candidate* directly references films that Capra directed. There is no evidence I am aware of to suggest this is the case. Rather, the visual imagery and story structures of Capra's films helped to generate a certain cinematic vernacular of film and story conventions.[25] It is knowledge of these conventions and how they function, rather than explicit reference to any film, story or character, which signals the lineage from *Mr. Deeds Goes to Town* to *The Manchurian Candidate*.[26] This appearance of cinematic and broader cultural conventions does not in any way undermine building a theory of cinematic authorship and expression on a theory of communication – it supports it. The production of a film like *The Manchurian Candidate* requires authorial competency to understand how to communicate using cinematic conventions to express meaning. *The Manchurian Candidate* is a film that intentionally attacks McCarthyism as an un-American and dangerous adventure. Its significance stems from the manner in which it resonates with a body of American films that established the basic ideological foundation on which a film like *The Manchurian Candidate* could be built.

Throughout this chapter I demarcate authorial from narrative voices in film to clarify the film author's role in filmic communication. A key component of this approach involves separating narration from visual representation. Visual representation and the construction of both the story and its narrator are authorial concerns. The telling of the story is the domain of this fictional narrator. By separating authorship and narration in this manner I am able to alleviate the problem that motivates poststructuralists' distrust of intention. Intention constrains the *meaning* of a film (although absolute fidelity between meaning and understanding is not required), but not its wider *significance*. Understanding the meaning of a film is essential. If a spectator has not understood the meaning, he or she has not understood the film. But meaning is only a part of interpretation. The significance of a film relates to the manner in which it engages with other films, public ideas and a wide range of socio-cultural matters. Spectators will make these connections *because of* the social and cultural competencies they share with authors. Filmmaking involves using the conventions of the medium to convey stories, ideas and a range of attitudes to a body of spectators who possess sufficient competency to understand these conventions. But just as language cannot be fully constrained in expression, neither can the use of film conventions. This does not justify abandoning authors or intentions because both are essential for understanding and judging films. Instead, this allows a space for spectators to invest their own interests into films in a manner that *engages with* authors' intentions.

4   CINEMATIC EXPRESSION

The historical period in academic film studies that witnessed the 'death of the author' also witnessed the ascendance of feminist film theory, followed soon after by studies of the politics and representation of race and sexuality. Poststructuralism provided a critical standpoint that enabled a variety of critics to make evident the systematic patriarchal, white, heterosexual bias of dominant film production and wider cultural practices. Constance Penley notes:

> the convergence of film and feminism with a new and forceful reading, on the one hand, of ideological determinations, and, on the other, of the Freudian emphasis on the relation of sexuality to language and image, could not have been more fortuitous, or its effects more productive ... Cinema, as a sort of microcosm, provided a model for the construction of subject positions in ideology, while its highly Oedipalised narratives lent themselves to a reading of the unconscious mechanisms of sexual difference in our culture. (1988: 3)

This 'fortuitous' convergence provided a means for diagnosing the underscoring gender bias in films by characterising their production in terms of a system rather than individual expression. But because the problem was seen to be systematic, there was no straightforward solution that could explain how Hollywood films could engage female pleasure, yet clearly some films were capable of doing so. A number of psychoanalytical analyses tackled the problem of how female spectators could find pleasure in a dominant text, but fewer considered how female pleasure could be structured into a film.

Two approaches in particular raised important issues for discussions of authorship. The first utilised the *Cahiers du cinéma* editors' approach that located auteurs in the excesses and ruptures in the film text. Whereas the *Cahiers du cinéma* editors were interested in capitalist economics, feminist film theorists applied this method to the ideology of gender. Claire Johnston, for example, contends that the films of Dorothy Arzner are progressive because they 'de-naturalise the workings of patriarchal ideology' (1988: 38). A film's 'internal tensions' ruptures it; 'instead of its ideology being simply assumed and virtually invisible, it is revealed and made explicit' (1988: 39). Arzner's films do not radically transform the ideological biases of commercial cinema, although they do make evident the problems and challenges to be confronted for a transformation in feminist filmmaking. The second approach poses a more radical solution. If, as feminist theorists have proposed, commercial cinema is inherently patriarchal, then other production methods must be sought. Pam Cook (1981) advocates harnessing small-scale, artisanal, avant-garde modes of production that, because they do not engage substantially with commercial interests, enable a greater degree of self-expression.

One approach that was explicitly dismissed by Johnston was to simply 'correct' the historical canon of filmmaking by identifying the numerous women that have been significant in the history of the medium. Seán Burke, discussing literary authorship, explains why. 'The very idea of the canon enables patriarchy to police the border between authorship and writing in hierarchical terms which have traditionally placed women "writers" in the second and devalued category' (1995b: 145). This is largely because 'the idea of authorship ... rested on a phallocentric picture of the autonomous creator consolidated in turn by criteria of aesthetic merit which were inadequate to the diversities of female experience' (ibid.). In the 1980s, though, the very notion of an 'authentic female experience was dismissed as essentialist and mystificatory, while the attempt to establish a female authorial canon was seen to do little more than recuperate women's writing for a moribund humanist aesthetic' (1995b: 146). Not surprisingly, this description characterises the situation with film well. It is reasonably easy to identify important directors such as Alice Guy, Elvira Notari, Germaine

Dulac, Esther Shub, Leni Riefenstahl and Dorothy Arzner, screenwriters like Anita Loos, Frances Marion and June Mathis, and even films aimed at female spectators, like those Mathis wrote for Rudolph Valentino. Canon revision misses the point, Johnston argues. To do so would simply mask significant historiographical issues, such as the power imbalances between the genders and the manifestations this has had on cultural production and expression. Revised canons would simply level male and female contributions to the history of the medium and would shift attention away from the patriarchal ideology and organisation of film production. The very premise of female subjectivity, as either object or process, would risk being lost to the empirical signs of inclusion in the historical record. An essentialist perspective would potentially equate women in the canon with the representation of female experience and remain silent on the nature of representation. There is a fundamental question of historiographic principles. The question is about not just a more balanced historical record, but also the method of writing film history that excluded women in the first place (see Johnston 1988: 37).

These arguments make clear the fundamental issue of expression in a conception of authorship. In this chapter I will explore the notion of expression in film production through gender, institutions, race and autobiography. These are only a few of the possible topics, but will be sufficient to elaborate the importance and dynamics of intention and expression in film production and reception. To do so, there are two principal assumptions that I will challenge. First, dominant commercial film production reproduces patriarchal, white, heterosexual, capitalist ideologies. I do not doubt that this is often true, but question that this has ever been necessarily true of commercial filmmaking and its narratives, or any mode of filmmaking. A historiographically sophisticated analysis of production will likely produce a more responsive understanding of ideological limitations than a theoretical model that imposes a master narrative (such as all Hollywood narratives are Oedipal). Second, expression and intention have been aligned with a Romantic conception of authorship that asserts a god-like control over meaning. The model of authorship outlined in the previous chapter avoids this problem. By separating meaning from significance, I maintain that authors intentionally produce texts while not fully determining the way that they can be read. Also, by abandoning subject-centred reason for communicative, or intersubjective reason, I locate the conventions for

In *Scorpio Rising* (1964) Kenneth Anger examines narcissistic youth worshipping a morbid popular culture

cinematic expression as shared territory for the filmmaker and spectator. Successful communication in film presumes the author and spectator each possess sufficient competency to produce and understand respectively the representational strategies used in the film. These representational strategies are not fixed, but evolve in response to the needs and broader social experiences of the people who use them.

This notion of expression is at one and the same time obvious and extremely difficult to explain. In *Scorpio Rising* (1964) Kenneth Anger expresses a critique of a narcissistic youth culture built on the mythologies of popular culture. To communicate this message there must also be a body of spectators with adequate competency in experimental films to understand the filmmaker's intention. It is not so straightforward to state that John Schlesinger, or any other individual member of the production team, expresses concerns about urban social decay in *Midnight Cowboy* (1969). One obvious reason relates to the conditions of production. Experimental filmmaking typically involves a degree of individual control over a film not available to commercial films with large production crews and financial obligations. Collaborative commercial production does not equate to ideological determinism, though. The system of negotiation involved in production and collective authorship simply disperses the location of the film's expression(s) across relevant individuals, but generally not equally. Both films are expressive, but we

Urban decay reflects social decay in *Midnight Cowboy* (1969)

cannot attribute expression to Schlesinger as we can with Anger, at least not without evidence of his singular control over the film's meaning. This distinction between experimental and commercial filmmaking is more of a strong tendency than an absolute boundary. Experimental film is typically free of many of the constraints experienced by commercial filmmaking, but must still communicate with its audience.

Tom Gunning has argued on a number of occasions that the changes in narrative film practices between 1908 and 1913 should not be seen as a development in film towards an essential storytelling capacity, but a shift in balance from one mode of filmmaking to another. Early films, he notes, exploit the notion of the spectacle. Georges Méliès constructs a flat, proscenium-like image wonderfully suited to tricks like the decapitations and recapitations in *Le Bourreau Turc* (*The Terrible Turkish Executioner*, 1904),

Méliès' trick of removing his head, attaching it to wires and growing another in *The Melomaniac* (1903)

or the multiple singing heads produced by multiple exposures in *Le Mélomane* (*The Melomaniac*, 1903). Countless early films directly address the audience, colluding with them, such as the Pathé brothers' *Par le Trou de Serrue* (*Peeping Tom*, 1901), Biograph's *From Show Girl to Burlesque Queen* (1903), G. A. Smith's *Mary Jane's Mishap* (1903) and the Edison Manufacturing Company's *The Great Train Robbery* (1903). Other films, such as panoramas and train journeys, elaborate the notion of the photographic image with motion, in films like Auguste and Louis

From Show Girl to Burlesque Queen (1903): the show girl acknowledges the presence of the film audience

Lumière's *Départ de Jérusalem en Chemin de Fer* (*Leaving Jerusalem by Railway*, 1896), Biograph's *The Georgetown Loop* (1903) or the Edison Manufacturing Company's *Pan-American Exposition by Night* (1901) and *Skyscrapers of New York City* (1903). These films present an experience of modernity through cinematic motion, compression and expansion of time, disjunctions of space, fragmentation of the human body, and direct audience address. Ben Singer contends that early film, as spectacle, provided a train-

The Georgetown Loop (1903) provides spectators with an experience of rail travel in a picturesque location

ing ground for spectators retaining a memory of an environment not fully succumbed to the shocks and stimuli of urban modernity (1995: 94). The period from 1908 to 1913 saw a shift in commercial filmmaking. Cinema as spectacle became subordinate to the narrative and dramatic logic of a story. The direct audience address was abandoned for a closed drama with a cinematic fourth wall firmly in place. Shots such as panoramas, which had been spectacles in and of themselves, both for what they showed and the manner in which the space was explored, became subordinate to narrative logic. The audience experience during this period in film history shifted from participant, of sorts, in a scene, to a viewer of one. Early films were entertaining, but not principally escapist.

It is this aesthetic and audience address that the American avant-garde cinema revisited from the 1940s onwards. It would be a mistake, though, to suggest that avant-garde filmmakers simply picked up where early filmmakers left off. Early cinema was principally a commercial entertainment:

> Certainly early filmmakers envisioned no aesthetic project like that of the avant-garde filmmaker. It is dubious that any of these films were thought about aesthetically at all. However, they display quite nakedly new relations to the representation of space that the camera made possible. Some of these possibilities were rediscovered by the avant-garde. But every rediscovery is a recreation. In this case tasks and roles that were unimaginable to the filmmakers of cinema's first decade are implied. (Gunning 1983: 365)

Gunning views the relationship between early and avant-garde cinema in aesthetic terms in order to help to explain the visual logic of many American avant-garde films, and to rescue early films 'from the ghetto of primitive babbling to which the progress-oriented model of film history has assigned them' (1983: 355). He further notes that both early and avant-garde cinemas differ from commercial narrative cinema, but each does so differently. Early film did not have commercial narrative filmmaking as an aesthetic option against which to react. Many early films address their historical period symptomatically rather than engage it thematically. Avant-garde filmmakers, in contrast, rely on early films precisely because of what they view as their anti-illusionist aesthetic. This distinction is rooted in the filmmaker's role. Early filmmakers could be very inventive, but it would be a stretch in most cases to think of them as artists. Early filmmaking developed out of a range of cultural antecedents and existing exhibition practices and had a distinctly economic incentive. Films were seen as commodities to be sold by the foot and run until they were no longer economically valuable. Preservation of early films is mainly a consequence of luck, copyright submissions and critical bias about authorship. Mid-century American avant-garde filmmakers were able to recognise in these films numerous symptomatic representations of the experience of the modern world: the spectacle, speed, malleability of time and space, tensions between surface and depth. Their lineage as visual stimuli helped to foster analogies in experimental films with poetry rather than the novel (see James 1989: 29). Film itself, being able to record and alter the image of reality, capable of compressing together two disparate spaces, of changing the experience of time, is *the* modern medium, as Dziga Vertov (1984) repeatedly exclaimed. This is one of the underscoring formalist principles of mid-century American avant-garde filmmaking. Attempts to investigate the properties of film were about not just understanding the medium, but also exploring modernity itself. This is one of the important distinctions between avant-garde and commercial cinemas: commercial narratives present allegories *of* the modern world, avant-garde films frequently constitute meditations *on* it.

This notion of avant-garde filmmaker as poet, stepping out of the confines of an impure form of filmmaking, has a clear ring of the Romantic notion of an author. In as far as avant-garde filmmakers set themselves off from conventional film production, proclaim a poetry of film, and rely upon the notion of self-expression, this *seems* a fair assertion. The Romantic author is conceived of as that solitary and unique genius external to society and innately inspired to artistic feats. We need, though, to be careful about the veracity of statements distinguishing commercial from experimental filmmakers. Andrew Bennett is right that the Romantic author is a remarkably troublesome notion: 'There is no reason why the genius is able to create the works that he creates' (2005: 60). Bennett's statement signals a problem about the conceptualisation of authorship, not the act of authorship itself. To suggest that experimental filmmakers are inspired to create visionary works almost unconsciously and transcendentally mystifies the very real principles on which these filmmakers work. 'The paradox is that while Romantic poetics focus on authorship, they also evacuate authorship of subjectivity' (Bennett 2005: 65). Experimental films do not come from nowhere, but develop from mental engagement with issues of film form, aesthetics, ideology, philosophy, vision, myth, non-conscious states of mind and lived experiences, to name just a few obvious concerns. It is the very subjectivity of the filmmaker(s) that gives a work any coherence it has and presents that work as something to be understood, be this intellectually or emotionally.

Pam Cook argues that by its very nature of production artisanal filmmaking enables self-expression that inherently opposes the concerns of capitalist economics. It also, Cook argues, limits the constraints on expression that come with commercial obligations. This is important enough for experimental filmmakers, but Cook has further concerns. Artisan film production is custom fit for feminist filmmakers. Self-expression

> is a concept which, with its emphasis on the personal, the intimate, and the domestic, has always been important to the Women's Movement, and the personal diary form, for instance, has always been a means of self-expression for women to whom other avenues were closed. The suppression of the 'personal', albeit politically correct, brings to the surface specific problems and contradictions for women, and for feminist filmmakers. (Cook 1981: 272)

This capacity for self-expression is not unimpeded. Although there can be a great deal of freedom from commercial obligations, there are nevertheless other institutional influences that arise from systems of funding and patronage. State sponsored filmmaking, for instance, often incorporates, implicitly or explicitly, political agendas of the time. These issues can range from policies for aesthetic education to the manner in which the nation is represented. Arts funding councils need to justify and account for the public money spent. When selecting projects to be produced, funding councils must also be mindful of the needs and practices of other arts institutions and especially commercial film and television industries.[1]

David E. James also notes the centrality of women's filmmaking in the cinematic avant-garde. This provided an avenue for expression that did more than present alternative voices, but in the context of shifting sexual mores following World War Two, brought to the foreground the full range of women's concerns, 'especially the politics of domestic life and parturition. In their attention to female sexuality they reproduced the aesthetics and rituals of their subcultural location, taking to its logical extreme a main function of the underground' (1989: 314). Feminist film-makers were not the only group of experimental filmmakers to highlight sexuality. Homosexuality, especially male homosexuality, also featured significantly in postwar avant-garde films. It is not surprising that female sexuality and homosexuality should play such a significant role in avant-garde filmmaking, given the repression of anything but a masculine notion of heterosexuality in Hollywood narratives throughout the history of the Production Code. Carolee Schneemann's film *Fuses* (1964–68) demon-strates just how complex and engaging artisanal film production can be. James notes that this film responds directly to two films Stan Brakhage made about Schneemann's relationship with musician James Tenney: *Loving* (1957) and *Cat's Cradle* (1959). It engages a number of concerns, such as sexual expression in commercial film, female sexuality within heterosexual congress and feminist perspectives on the representation of sexual intercourse. Despite this, the film proved difficult for feminists to accept, as James indicates: 'its explicitness appeared anti-feminist in the context of feminist attempts to differentiate erotica from pornography, and its fascination with the male as much as with the female body was unusual outside homosexual pornography' (1989: 318).

In *Fuses*, Schneemann undermines the conventional strategies of gender representation in both pornography and conventional cinema. The film's structure resists the teleology of male ejaculation. The time of the film is not the time of the sexual act, but of the ecstatic moment. There is no beginning or end of the act, only of the film. The imagery jumps between sexual acts, leaves, running on the beach, the cat, and so forth. Male and female genitalia are equally represented, and there is no singular point of view. The images of nudity and the sexual act are often edited rapidly. Schneemann substantially affects the surface of the image, by scratching, toning and in many ways deteriorating it, as well as superimposing shots, sprocket holes and punched frames at the ends of reels over the sexual acts.[2] In many shots the lighting and focus deny the spectator little more than an outline. She does not generally linger on images of either body, denying the audience voyeuristic pleasures. The film also acknowledges the presence of its spectator in a way that classical narrative construc-tion does not. Affecting and distorting the surface of the image evokes historical awareness of the representation of sexuality and the sexual act itself. The scratching suggests a film that has been run many times previously; the projection of the film, like the act, is both unique and rooted in previous encounters. Each encounter is a variation, continuation, and yet distinct. By manipulating the surface of the image and denying an objectified viewing position, Schneemann also causes the spectator to consider both the surface and depth of the image, prompting an awareness of the psychical depth of the sexual act rooted in the very surface of touch. Few films present such a detailed representation of personal experience. Schneemann shot most of the film herself (Tenney helped with some of the camerawork), edited it, and with her partner performed in it. As a result of the artisanal mode of production, there is little or no interference between Schneemann's intention and the film's realisation. She retains a moral responsibility for the work because it represents her individual intended meaning. The question of Schneemann's insightfulness or irresponsibility regarding the representation of female sexuality is ultimately a debate for the significance of the film in its wider socio-cultural contexts.

Maya Deren and Alexander Hammid offer a different type of film to consider. *Meshes of the Afternoon* (1943) is a dramatic representation of a dream. A few incidental events and objects that a woman (played by Deren, while Hammid photographed the film) registers on the way home and inside her house begin to multiply and twist in her afternoon dream. Simple things like picking up a flower, a man ahead on the road, dropping a key, a knife in a loaf of bread and a telephone off the hook recompile in the dream. The film has a cyclical form. The events and locations of objects differ each time, as do their purposes within the dream. As the dream progresses the woman duplicates herself in the dream. With each cycle, she sees herself from all the previous cycles, but again her position in the dream differs each time. The last full cycle is a waking dream. The man enters and wakes the woman, and they head upstairs. Everything is back in its place, but once upstairs, the woman's continued dream state again becomes evident, as she slashes at his face with a knife. His face becomes a mirror and breaks, and the broken pieces land on a beach. The final sequence does not complete its cycle. As in the previous cycle, the man has now become significant. We are still presented with the flower, the steps and the same entrance to the house, although this time it is the man rather than the woman that enters. His gaze pans the room and ends on the woman, a piece of broken mirror in her hand, apparently having cut her own throat. To conclude that this has been a suicide, though, is inaccurate. The repetition of objects and the presence of the man in the previous cycle, aided by the misplaced flower from her lap, as she enters sleep, to the steps outside the house as he enters, leaves the end of the film ambiguous. Deren maintained that this film

> does not record an event which could be witnessed by other persons. Rather, it reproduces the way in which the sub-conscious of an individual will develop, interpret and elaborate an apparently simple and causal incident into a critical emotional experience. (Quoted in Sitney 2002: 9)

The filmmakers do not make a clear point with this film, nor do they aim to. Deren explicitly defended the view that the film resists psychoanalytical reading and narrative closure. The filmmakers aimed to create, as Deren insists, a mythological experience rather than a narrative one (in Sitney 2002: 11).

Deren indicates that one of the core problems the film faced was the distance between this intention and audience interpretation habits. 'When it was made, however, there was no anticipation of the general audience and no experience of how the dominant cultural tendency toward personalised psychological interpretation could impede the understanding of the film' (quoted in Sitney 2002: 11). Stated otherwise, the film could too easily be read through more conventional narrative codes and cultural connotations that aimed at locating closure and meaning. This produced misreadings of the film. Robert Sklar notes this as a general problem for trance films and a reason that they were abandoned at the end of the 1950s (see 1994: 310). The reception problems Deren and Sklar identify point to a broader lack of spectator competency due to the absence of representational convention. These films appeared more as a private mode of expression. Where convention lacks, other publicly available keys for interpretation prevail. If intention were not relevant for reception, then we would have to accept that *Meshes of the Afternoon* is a film about a suicide. This is not the film that Deren and Hammid made. Once suitably prompted, spectators are able to understand the film as intended.

The Romantic notion of film authorship is difficult to resist when confronted with a filmmaker like Stan Brakhage, who epitomises this Romantic self-conception of the poetic filmmaker.[3] Brakhage, in his films, frequently interrogates basic concerns of his own existence, such as birth, marriage, family, sex and death, as both lived experiences and philosophical questions. The personal significance and assertion of ownership of these concerns are usually marked by the words 'by Brakhage' scratched into the film and presented as an animated signature. James contends Brakhage 'made filmmaking the agency of his being. Bridging the aesthetic and existential, film became identified with his life and coextensive with it, simultaneously his vocation and avocation, his work and play, his joy and terror – as integral as breathing' (1989: 37). Ownership for Brakhage is not a commercial concern, but a subjective claim. Most of Brakhage's films are about vision, or as James puts it, the 'autobiography of perception' (1989: 44). Significantly, with vision Brakhage does not aim to reproduce the visible world realistically. He maintains instead that our perception of the world is structured by our conceptions of it:

> Imagine an eye unruled by man-made laws of perspective, an eye unprejudiced by compositional logic, an eye which does not respond to the name of everything but which must know each object encountered in life through an adventure of perception. How many colors are there in a field of grass to the crawling baby unaware of 'Green'? How many rainbows can light create for the untutored eye? How aware of variations in heat waves can that eye be? Imagine a world alive with incomprehensible objects and shimmering with an endless variety of movement and innumerable gradations of color. Imagine a world before the 'beginning was the word'. (2001: 12)

It is this quest for pure vision that underscores much of Brakhage's work. His films do not show us pure vision, but provide a way of conceiving or imagining it. The paradox of his approach is that this objective of untainted vision is rendered through both his existence and through myth. *Dog Star Man* is, among many other things, a Sisyphusian parable of a man, Brakhage, climbing a mountain to fell a tree. To construct a linear narrative, even an existential narrative, out of the film is to miss the point, though. He requires of his films a different spectator from the one David Bordwell postulates for classical cinema. The film involves a vast array of techniques, including multiple superimposed layers of film, anamorphic lenses being twisted, scratching and baking the film, painting directly on to the film, dying it and even overlaying objects onto the film, especially fragments of other strips of film. For Brakhage the material filmstrip is as important as the images imprinted on it. While the camera treats the film at the level of the frame, the filmmaker need not. Brakhage's manipulation of the film runs across vast numbers of frames, disrupting the animation of any profilmic object. In *Mothlight* (1963), Brakhage removes the camera entirely. He constructs this film by attaching bits of dead moths and plants to clear film leader. Any animation in the resultant image is purely arbitrary and results only because of the discrepancy between the mode of construction and exhibition. In *Dog Star Man,* Brakhage's manipulation of the material film itself brings the depth of the image into conflict with its flat surface. This produces a range of effects. In some cases the resultant images possess a painterly quality. In others they frustrate the act of seeing the profilmic object, or a straightforward reading of the image. The tension between *film as strip* and *film as frame* prompts the viewer to consider the very process of a visual understanding through film by identifying the manner in which film projection reanimates still frames. Despite all of Brakhage's assertions about the artist, and his advocation of amateur production as a means of economic, aesthetic and intellectual emancipation, Sklar concludes reasonably that Brakhage 'avoided tendencies toward authoritarianism in the Romantic idea of the visionary artist, and reaffirmed the social as an integral part of the personal, and the democratic as an essential element of the cinema avant-garde' (1994: 310–2).

Although narrative and avant-garde cinemas pursued radically different aesthetic projects, they did not differ over a film's capacity to be used for expressive and discursive purposes. To help to demonstrate this I will examine *The Birth of a Nation*, directed by D. W. Griffith and co-written with Frank E. Woods, and two films produced allegedly in response to this film's notoriety: *Intolerance* (1916), written and directed by Griffith, and *Within Our Gates* (1920), written and directed by Oscar Micheaux. *The Birth of a Nation* is undoubtedly an exceptional work of narrative filmmaking, but is equally racist and offensive. Black and mulatto characters in the film are, for the most part, depicted as malicious and villainous. It did not help matters that key black characters were played by blacked-up white actors. Griffith's justification, reported by William K. Everson, that on the

A crowd of black actors in *The Birth of a Nation* (1915), a film with no leading roles for black performers

West Coast there were not enough black actors to play principal black characters is rather unconvincing, as is his defence that he was utilising the theatrical convention of the black-faced minstrel (see Everson 1998: 86). The vast number of black extras in the film suggests that black actors may not have been so hard to come by, although they may have lacked experience in screen acting. Similarly, to suggest that Griffith's minstrel casting was in deference to theatrical traditions contradicts the efforts he made to move cinema away from stage conventions. Griffith offered an economic argument also, noting that actors playing white characters could also be blacked-up to play black characters. The reverse was not an option, as black actors could not be whitened-up to play white characters. Although a more plausible argument, it seems a little suspect given the budget of the film. Lary May offers a more plausible explanation for Griffith's racist casting. For Griffith, 'Negroes were seen as innately dangerous: in spite of their potential for noble deeds, they could never really be trusted. Griffith thus forbid any "black blood" among the players who might have to touch white actresses' (1983: 83). Even more troublesome than mere villainous black characters are the economic and physical, especially sexual, threats they present to the white characters. The fear of black voting rights and the destruction of racial purity expressed in the film – already embodied in the mulatto characters – ignores the fact that mixed-race children were more frequently the result of consensual reproduction and white males raping black female slaves than black males raping white women. The melodramatic distinction between good and evil is, in the film, basically a question of black and white. The mulattos do not introduce a grey area, but are deemed black, denoting distinctions like white and non-white, pure and impure, civilised and uncivilised. This depiction is rooted in the entire aesthetic palette of the film, including the lighting, acting styles, costumes, positions of black characters in the sets and titles that mark these characters as having a limited grasp of language. Not surprisingly, *The Birth of a Nation* met fierce opposition from the National Association for the Advancement of Colored People (NAACP) and 'was banned in five states and nineteen cities' (Bogle 2001: 15). Additionally, as Lary May notes, the film caused severe problems for the National Board of Review. The Board, headed by Frederic Howe, in alliance with the NAACP, insisted on cuts to some of the most racist elements, yet Howe was still so disturbed by the film that he resigned his presidency (see 1983: 82–3). About the best we could say of Griffith's racial politics in this film is he was working from racist source material – Thomas W. Dixon's novel and stage play *The Clansman* (1905) – and reflecting the widespread white racism of the time.[4]

The controversy over *The Birth of a Nation* baffled Griffith. He did not appear to fully appreciate the nature of the offence he had caused with this film. Instead, as May indicates, Griffith saw the concerns over racism as an alibi for Republican reformers that had always been critical of his filmmaking. This was not helped when in February 1915 the Supreme Court, considering *Mutual Film Corporation v. Ohio Industrial Commission*, a case brought over Ohio's banning of *The Birth of a Nation*, ruled that the motion picture industry constituted a business rather than an agent of public opinion and therefore was not protected as free speech (see Koszarski 1994: 199–201). In 1916 Griffith addressed this concern over free speech in two works: a pamphlet entitled 'The Rise and Fall of Free Speech in America' and his epic film *Intolerance*. Initially Griffith had intended to release an early twentieth-century urban drama entitled *The Mother and the Law*, but instead vastly expanded this project, developing three historical storylines to complement the contemporary parable: the fall of Babylon, the St. Bartholomew's Day Massacre in France in 1572 and Christ's crucifixion. These multiple narratives, intercut with each other to highlight the thematic concerns shared across the storylines, added a new dimension to Griffith's already highly developed editing and narrative construction. Each story develops from conflict initiated by hate and intolerance, and is motivated by greed, betrayal, indifference and dogma – basically, any illiberal mindset that would seek power and authority, even at the cost of justice, reason and compassion. In all the historical stories intolerance is victorious: Cyrus lays siege to and defeats Babylon in an unprovoked attack; the Catholic French Crown slaughters the Huguenots; and Christ is crucified on the cross. The film's hope, and Griffith's point, pivots on the modern narrative. The Boy, sentenced to be executed for a murder

Intolerance (1916): The Dear One (Mae Marsh) and The Kindly Policeman (Tom Wilson) race to catch the Governor (Ralph Lewis)

The Dear One and The Kindly Policeman present the real killer, The Friendless One (Miriam Cooper), to the Governor

he did not commit, is about to be hanged. The Kindly Policeman visits the scene of the crime, believing a miscarriage of justice has been done, and discovers that that The Boy is most likely innocent. The Governor nevertheless refuses to stay the execution. The real murderer, The Friendless One, is found and The Dear One and The Kindly Policeman again race off to the Governor, who has just set off on a train. They manage to stop the train and present the murderer to the Governor. The Governor accepts the guilty plea of The Friendless One, and grants the stay. Unfortunately, the execution is about to take place and it appears doubtful if the stay will reach the gallows in time. A masterful piece of editing draws together both the resolution to the narrative and the film's main theme. Halting the execution not only prevents an injustice, but also breaks the cycle of intolerance perpetuated in all the other storylines. The modern storyline introduces hope. Prior to *Intolerance*, one of Griffith's main cinematic achievements was his internally coherent, realist narratives held together by the narrator's perspective on and moral judgements about the story (see Gunning 1991: 27–8). By intercutting across storylines, stitching them together with the repeated, linking image of 'The Woman that Rocks the Cradle', and in conjunction with the film's epilogue, Griffith reasserts his authorial presence. *Intolerance* is a remarkable film, yet, for all its qualities, the film's point seems muddled, providing no clear perspective on the issues of free speech and race that motivated the escalation of the film's scale in the first place.

With *Within Our Gates* Oscar Micheaux also did not address *The Birth of a Nation* directly. It is not even certain that Micheaux produced *Within Our Gates* as a direct response to *The Birth of a Nation*, although as Jane

Gaines points out, W. E. B. Du Bois, the writer, activist and co-founder of the NAACP, had, with other black leaders:

> called upon the African-American community to produce their own films in reply to the Dixon-Griffith epic, and it is not an exaggeration to say that a number of the first 'race movie' producers were acting in part out of a desire to correct the film's misrepresentations. (2001: 70)

Intolerance (1916): His innocence proven, The Boy (Robert Harron) is reunited with The Dear One

Micheaux took up this challenge and aimed *Within Our Gates* directly at the type of racial misrepresentations epitomised in Griffith's film. Micheaux produced a scenario and film that depicts African-Americans as normal, middle-class citizens. The film also portrays racial integration as an unremarkable, daily occurrence, but warns of the threat that small-minded racists present, and the realities in the 1910s and early 1920s of lynching. It undermines a film like *The Birth of a Nation* by presenting as irrational and dangerous the fear that certain spheres of white society have of black and mulatto citizens. Like *The Birth of a Nation*, *Within Our Gates* is a family melodrama that examines the distinct racial attitudes between the American north and south and highlights a number of the concerns that *The Birth of a Nation* glosses over. *Within Our Gates* tells the story of Sylvia, a mulatto teacher in a southern school for black children. The local black population struggles to pay for their most basic needs, let alone schooling. Families pay what they can for the education of their children, but this does not cover costs and the school is threatened with closure. Sylvia travels north to raise funds. On her travels she meets a black doctor, Dr Vivian, and a rich white philanthropist, Mrs Ella Warwick. Mrs Warwick pledges $5000 for the school. Upon being pressed by her friend to withdraw the pledge, on the grounds that blacks have no need of education, Mrs Warwick increases her pledge tenfold. When smitten Dr Vivien calls looking for Sylvia, her cousin, Alma, tells him the story of Syliva's past, which we are shown in a prolonged flashback.

Sylvia helps her foster father, Jasper Landry, with his sharecropping accounts, and discovers that the white plantation owner, Philip

Within Our Gates (1920): A dramatic shot of the beam from which Jasper Landry (William Stark) and his wife (Mattie Edwards) are lynched

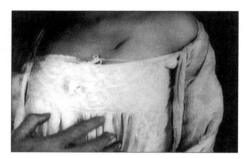

Armand Gridlestone (Grant Gorman) assaults Sylvia (Evelyn Preer)

Gridlestone, has been cheating him. Landry visits Gridlestone to settle the sharecropping accounts. Micheaux avoids a basic antagonism between the white plantation owner and the under-educated sharecropper by including white sharecroppers on the plantation and by having the plantation owner cheat them also. A white sharecropper shoots and kills Gridlestone through an open window. However, Gridlestone had seen the white sharecropper and pulls out a pistol before he is shot. In the commotion, Gridlestone's gun ends up in Landry's hand. Efram, Gridlestone's black servant, saw Landry in Gridlestone's office and accuses him of the murder. Sylvia and her family go into hiding, but are found and her foster parents lynched. While this is happening, Armand Gridlestone, Philip Gridlestone's brother, accosts Sylvia. Armand places a hand on Sylvia's breast and sees her scar. He realises he is about to rape his own daughter. The taboo of incest is sufficient to stop Armand from assaulting Sylvia further. Jane Gaines provides a provocative analysis of this sequence:

> It is as though Micheaux was reconstructing [Reconstruction era] history in the scene and foregrounding the sexual secrets left out in *The Birth of a Nation*. For never once does that film intimate that the very mulatto class it wants to discredit is the product of the indiscretion of the men of the planter class. (2001: 74)

The assault concludes with the intertitle 'A scar on her chest saved her because, once it was revealed, Gridlestone knew that Sylvia was his daughter – his legitimate daughter from a marriage to a woman of her race – who was later adopted by the Landrys'. Gaines notes that there are questions about the accuracy of the English titles in this copy of the film.[5] A review of the film's premiere contradicts the view that Sylvia was legitimate, and this corresponds with Micheaux's promotional literature. Whether this intertitle is accurate or not is unclear, so it is worth looking at the implication of both cases. If Sylvia is illegitimate then Armand is simply a villain. His attack on Sylvia's mother is rooted in cultural and legal biases: 'since African-American women were characterised as sexually willing it was difficult to argue they had ever been raped or sexually assaulted' (Gaines 2001: 75). The mere existence of mulatto children in the south, born of white, plantation males and black female slaves, strongly suggests that the rape of black women was not *seen* as a crime within white society, but likely both recreation and a means for increasing slave numbers. If, on the other hand, Armand and Sylvia's mother did marry, then Armand and Sylvia's mother would have committed miscegenation. This was certainly taboo and even illegal in some states, especially, but not only, in the south. If the existing titles are accurate, then Micheaux has taken the evidence of mulatto offspring and posed a dilemma to the censors and to audiences: are these children the consequence of rape or miscegenation? (see Gaines 2001: 78). It is precisely this question of justice and values that Griffith's mastery of film form, dramatic narrative and Victorian sensibility distorts.

Micheaux does not level an attack on white society. Throughout the film, as Gaines notes, 'Micheaux's heroes and heroines are wronged by their own people. The characters in Micheaux are "hell-bent" on causing trouble for one another, but not because they are inherently evil' (2001: 78). While an accurate statement, it is problematically worded. *Within Our Gates* problematises the very notion of one's 'own people'. Sylvia is half-black, half-white. In Boston she is aided by a wealthy white woman, engaged to a black doctor and betrayed by her black relatives. She moves back and forth between the north and south. At one and the same time Sylvia belongs to both races, and to neither. In the United States, the notion of *one drop of black blood* was (and is) often used to define and self-define someone as black, while at times the lighter skin tones of mulattos excludes them from this racial alignment. Through this film Micheaux appears to be prompting the audience to abandon the myth of racial purity and incompatibilities. By creating a contemporary narrative, as opposed to Griffith's historical narrative, Micheaux signals the need to embrace racial integration as a social reality and uproot racial fears ingrained in cultural mythology.

In contrast, a writer/director like Bill Douglas presents a less polemical approach to filmmaking in his trilogy *My Childhood* (1972), *My Ain Folk* (1973) and *My Way Home* (1978). Covering the period from Douglas's childhood through to early adulthood, these films illustrate extreme post-World War Two poverty in Newcraighall, a mining village on the edge of Edinburgh, and later National Service duty in Egypt. Being fictionalised accounts of Douglas's youth, these films could easily be underestimated simply as autobiographical films. While these *are* autobiographical films, they are more than mere illustrations of Douglas's life. They instead illustrate themes of human brutality and kindness synecdochically through Douglas's fictional surrogate, Jamie. The films portray these themes not so

My Childhood (1972): Jamie's coal

much through narrative development, but isolated vignettes and image composition. There is, for the most part, a complete elision of cause and effect structures. Many scenes could be interchanged without detriment, but not the order of shots. Precise framings convey specific aesthetic information that informs interpretation across the film. Two well-discussed instances from *My Childhood* will help to illustrate this strategy.

In the first scene Jamie returns home, having been out looking for coal. His cousin Tommy, with whom he lives, is chopping up a wooden chair and scrunching up wallpaper to fuel the fire. It is clear that they burn anything for fuel, including their own belongings. Jamie empties his pockets, placing four pieces of coal on the kitchen table. He then states 'I'm hungry'. Tommy responds by calling Jamie selfish, knocks the coal onto the floor and attacks him. The boys' grandmother tries to break up the fight. The sequence ends with peace restored and all three sitting by the fire. Tommy, sitting beside Jamie, extends his arm around him. In the second scene, which follows shortly

Jamie (Stephen Archibald), Tommy (Hughie Restorick) and their Grandmother (Jean Taylor Smith) warm themselves by the fire

after, Tommy has taken wilted poppies from his mother's grave, brought them home and placed them in a cup of water on the table. Jamie returns later with a kettle of hot water. Tommy is not in the room. Jamie's actions are memorable because they seem so incongruous. He dumps the flowers and water on the floor, replaces the cup and proceeds to overfill it, allowing the water to spill onto the table and floor for a number of seconds. Jamie then lifts the cup, empties it onto the table, and goes to his grandmother, who is asleep in her rocking chair. Jamie places the warmed cup into her hands, and then proceeds to help keep her hands warm by wrapping his hands around hers.

Tommy's poppies as still life

Either Jamie's fight with his cousin or his warming his granny's hands could have been presented first. They are simply events in Jamie's life with no causal connection. The order of the images, though, could not be reversed. When Jamie returns in the first sequence, he opens the door and peers in before entering. There is then a cut to his optical point of view. He sees his granny's hands. This shot is then answered when he places the cup in her hands. No amount of dialogue could explain Jamie's love for her better. This shot of Jamie warming his granny's hands also causes us to re-evaluate our response to the earlier shot of Jamie spilling the water. Some scenes, as John Caughie indicates, 'have to be read backwards' (1993: 200). Caughie comments that Jamie's action of spilling the water 'shocks my bourgeois sense of domestic propriety' (1993: 201). Such shocks in the film effectively com-

Jamie overfills the cup

Jamie warms his grandmother's hands

My Childhood (1972): Point-of-view shot – Jamie sees his grandmother's hands

municate the extremes of the poverty Jamie experiences, as well as the relative values such poverty generates. Jamie's actions are no longer reckless; under the circumstances they are reasonable and compassionate. They cause us to abandon immediate and conventional understandings of his actions and re-evaluate Jamie's motivations and Douglas's intentions. Furthermore, the images of the coal and the flowers on the table suggest still life paintings. Instead of the typical images of abundance, like fruit, flowers or game, only a few lumps of coal and dead flowers are depicted. These are not melancholic images in the film. The film does not evoke pity, nor does it romanticise poverty. There is a beauty in these images, but also a brutal starkness. The film causes spectators to think about poverty, but avoids the polemics of Marxism on the one hand and character sentimentality on the other. As a consequence of this strategy, spectators re-evaluate their own values in light of what is presented onscreen.

Because Douglas was the writer/director, and the films are autobiographical, it seems reasonable to attribute to Douglas sole authorship of this trilogy. While undoubtedly the most significant person involved in their production, Douglas was not working in isolation. The evidence Andrew Noble (1993) uncovered in the British Film Institute files and in the correspondence of *My Ain Folk*'s editor, Peter West, provides invaluable information illustrating the intellectual contributions that helped to shift an autobiographical script into a trilogy for public consumption. Douglas's initial script for *My Childhood*, as Noble notes, relied on flashback. Lindsay Anderson recommended dropping the flashback, thereby altering substantially the film's narrative address, and changing the name of the film from *Jamie* to *My Childhood*. He also discussed the shoot with Douglas when Douglas had begun setting up camera positions (see 1993: 126). Even a small alteration like a change in title, as Mamoun Hassan (2008) mentions, changed a single film into a trilogy. As Noble reports, West, who took over editing *My Ain Folk* from Douglas, noted that Douglas's personal involvement in the film, so crucial for the scripting and shooting, was poisonous in the editing room. The film was rescued largely by Lindsay Anderson's recommendation that Douglas take a holiday, allowing West to finish editing the film (see 1993: 147–8). One may object that these interventions are minimal, and therefore trivial, at least as far as authorship of the trilogy is concerned. If we are only concerned with reading the films, there is likely no harm in talking about Douglas's film, or the way that Douglas frames a shot. This is not because he is the director, but because he exercised a great deal of control over the shooting. It is more questionable, for instance, to discuss shots in a Bergman film without considering Sven Nykvist's contributions. However, if instead we are concerned with the authorship of the *Bill Douglas Trilogy*, focusing only on Douglas mythologises the control of a writer/director and risks attributing to the director contributions he did not make. Only detailed research into the actual conditions of authorship allows for a rigorous assessment of contributions that can generate a more robust analysis of meaning and significance. According to Noble's account of the production history of the trilogy, without the contributions of some key individuals these films would have been incoherent.

Throughout this chapter I have focused on three principal concerns. First, even the most personal and poetic filmmaking does not justify the excesses of a Romantic conception of authorship. Films are public objects that communicate meaning. They are open to interpretation, critical judgement and evaluation within broader debates. These interpretations and judgements consider the work itself, and also the author or authors that remain accountable for the implications of the work. The case of *The Birth of a Nation* demonstrates that this question of accountability has a historical dimension. Authorship must be evaluated in the context of its own time and place. To properly understand and judge a film one must therefore be aware of the conventions and values of the period within which the film was made. While a Romantic understanding of authors is too limited, views that abandon authorship for critical engagement ignore both the responsibility authors have for their expressions and the basic principle that works are produced for reasons. Retaining the concept of intention allows an authored work to be considered as an act of communication and not simply an aesthetic object. Second, films do not come from nowhere. Whether engaged with political debates, aesthetics or institutions, films are necessarily inflected by external frameworks. Filmmakers, like all authors, work through institutions. This is fairly obvious for commercial production, but even avant-garde filmmakers who claim autonomy outside the film industry engage with funding bodies, galleries and festivals, and consider exhibition environments and audience knowledge and expectations. Lastly, films are frequently made collectively, even if this means only a camera operator and actor. With most films we should expect to find more than one individual significantly responsible for the film and the ideas it communicates. These contributors can include directors, writers, producers, cinematographers, sound designers, editors, set designers, actors, and so on. However, no individual role will guarantee anyone involved in a production an authorial position. Authorship is different from craftsmanship. To locate an author or authors in filmmaking is to locate who is responsible for building into a film its potentially complex structure of meanings. An automatic reliance on directors is, as I indicated anecdotally in the introduction to this book, sloppy scholarship. Authorship is a fact of production. Identifying the author or authors of a film is a historical and critical procedure aimed at illuminating this fact of production. Throughout the book I have focused mainly on what an author does. In the next chapter I will address what an author is.

5   INTENTION

Throughout this book I have focused on the role of the filmic author, but I have not explained what such an author is. Doing so is the task of this chapter. I have argued against approaches to film authorship that set aside real achievements by real individuals in favour of fictional entities like implied authors and author functions, and even abandon authors entirely while proclaiming 'the death of the author'. Commitment to actual authors is not new or even recently revived. While these theoretical challenges to empirical authorship were in full swing, historians and critics persisted in discussing films as if they were really made by real individuals, with little more than a passing nod to such theories. In the past twenty years this resistance to surrendering the empirical author has gained evidential and theoretical support. Film historians and archival researchers like Thomas Schatz (1988), Tom Gunning (1991) and Robert L. Carringer (1996) have uncovered extensive documentation about the production practices of individuals.[1] Literary theorists like E. D. Hirsch Jr (1967), Steven Knapp and Walter Benn Michaels (1985) and Jack Stillinger (1991) have re-examined the philosophical and theoretical foundations of authorship and intention. Stillinger goes beyond simply defending empirical authorship. He contends that all authorship, including literary authorship, is inherently collaborative. Philosophers and film theorists Paisley Livingston (1997 and 2009) and Berys Gaut (1997) have re-examined film authors as biological facts and film authorship as a frequently collaborative process. In this chapter

I build on these arguments, using John Searle's (1991) analysis of collective intentional action to explain how film can be both intentionally and collectively authored. I rely on the premise that authorship is essentially an empirical activity and that any theory of film authorship must be able to account for actual production conditions and inform historical research into filmmaking.

Before proceeding I need to clarify my use of the term 'intention'. The intentionalist/anti-intentionalist debate raised earlier focuses on the meaning of the text under consideration. It develops from concerns within criticism over the very real problem of whether an author's intended meaning should govern the reading of a text, or even if intended meaning is recoverable through reading. The views I endorse are those of E. D. Hirsch Jr. Hirsch agrees with the basic poststructuralist principle that language is polysemic (see 1984). Linguistic expressions in a natural language will typically not have a single meaning. However, poststructuralists see this polysemy as cause for relativism in interpretation and contend that it impedes working backwards through a text to identify the author's intent. An author's intention is not only irrecoverable, they maintain, but also undesirable. Language continually evolves, so the meanings that are possible in a text also evolve and multiply. To impose a sanctioned meaning undermines the fluidity of language. Hirsch disagrees with this position. He insists that the plurality of meanings possible *requires* authorial intent:

> No linguistic code can determine the meanings of a text, because linguistic codes by themselves are far too capacious and flexible to determine meanings for individual texts. Some special human agency or act is needed to decide upon the choice of a governing sub-code (i.e. the particular sub-system of conventions that shall determine textual meanings) ... The fact of interpretive disagreement *proves* the correctness of the basic insight that an act of choosing a sub-code is needed. The range of existing linguistic norms and conventions, by themselves, do not take care of the matter. (1984: 90; emphasis in original)

Between Hirsch's view and the views of poststructuralists is essentially the question of which sub-codes matter.

Any norm based merely on a principle, say, the most beautiful meaning, or the most relevant meaning, or the most socially useful meaning, etc., would imply a sub-code that is chosen by the *critic*. By contrast, the author-norm does not select a particular value norm as such. It offers allegiance to some past *person's* governing sub-code, no matter what its value principle turns out to be. (Ibid.; emphasis in original)

This author-norm is intent. Hirsch's argument poses a challenge for critics. Interpretation constitutes an investigation into the nature of authorial intent, not an imposition of pre-determined critical values that structure the interpretation of linguistic strings. This distinction between intention and interpretation does have practical problems. As poststructuralists contend, simply reading a text will likely not reveal which of all the possible readings is the intended reading. Hirsch accepts this, but again argues that this does not justify abandoning authorial meaning. Instead, it indicates the need to improve critical skills and treat interpretation as an empirical subject requiring research. 'An empirical subject is *a posteriori* in its essence. Its results are determined by a reality that is not constituted in advance by the investigator' (1984: 91).[2] Interpretation functions like any study open to improvements in evidence and the analysis of this evidence.

One of the problems for understanding authorship in film has been the imposition of critical concerns onto analyses of authorship. Authorship has been compounded with issues of aesthetic value, ideology and politics, for instance. These are all significant concerns, but *secondary* to the question of authorship itself. If we wish to understand artistic film authorship or the ideological implications of being the author of a Hollywood film, we must first have available a basic definition of film authorship. Only once we know what an author is can we consider what it may take to be an artistic one.[3] More fundamentally, proposing that film even has authors presupposes that we can have a general definition of authorship not dependent on any specific medium. We must understand what an author is before elaborating how one can author things like books, films and plays. Paisley Livingston, in his essay 'Cinematic Authorship', proposes a general definition of authorship worth considering:[4]

> Author = (def) the agent (or agents) who intentionally make(s) an utterance, where 'utterance' refers to any action, an intended function of which is expression or communication. (1997: 134)

This definition accommodates both single and multiple, or collaborative, authorship, but for the moment I will consider only single authorship. The issue of intention in multiple authorship raises additional challenges, which I will address later in the chapter. My immediate concern is to establish the most basic definition of authorship on which a definition of collaborative film authorship can be built. There are three important qualities to Livingston's definition that aid this task. First, it defines an author as someone (an agent) who acts purposefully. Second, it claims that authors make utterances. I will look closer at the concept of 'making an utterance' shortly, but for the moment 'making an utterance' can be considered as producing (or causing to be produced) markings or actions that can convey one's meanings, and may include such media as literature, films or even gestures. 'Meaning' should be understood broadly. In a film this could involve basic story elements, emotions, attitudes or a critical point that an author wishes to express. There is a danger here that the notion of 'utterance' can be interpreted too widely. To make an utterance does not include just anyone involved in the material production of a work. An amanuensis may literally write a novel, but that novel is not her or his utterance. This distinction will prove crucial for understanding film authorship as a collective practice. Third, the purpose of authoring is to express or communicate. This implies an audience and presumes that the utterance is conveyed in a manner that is understandable by the reader or audience. It does not imply that anyone *does* understand the work, only that it is capable of being understood.[5] Typically this will require competency in a language and/or conventions in visual representation.[6]

Livingston's definition is useful, but it does not offer an analysis of the most basic notion of authorship. Elaborating this notion of authorship will help to indicate why intention matters. The term 'author' refers also to 'an agent who is a cause of an event', as in 'he was greedy, and therefore the author of his own downfall'. Consider this scenario: Jake, having finished a telephone call on his mobile phone, hangs up and puts his phone in his pocket. As he does so, he accidentally hits a button and begins recording video of the inside of his pocket. In one sense Jake is the cause, and therefore the author, of this recording. This level of authorship does not involve intention, so it falls short of Livingston's definition, but the video that results from this intentionless act can be read. For instance, one could look at this recording of blackness as a metaphor for the existential empti-ness of Jake's soul. Alternatively, it could also be read as evidence of the opacity of denim. Without any intention, there is no guidance on how to read this video, or if it should even be read at all.[7] In fact, we shouldn't read it, because lacking intention it means nothing. Both proposed inter-pretations are critical impositions on the accidental video footage.[8] Novels and films are not produced by accident, so we will want to eliminate this level of authorship from our discussion. To do this we need to distinguish between 'authors' and 'intending authors'. Livingston's definition char-acterises 'intending authors'. Referring to 'intending authors' throughout the chapter will become linguistically clumsy, so I will simply use the term 'author' to refer to an 'intending author'. I have no further need to discuss 'the author as mere cause', so hopefully my linguistic simplification will not cause confusion.[9]

Livingston's definition requires some further explanation and tinkering. His use of the term 'utterance' differs from conventional usage of the term in film studies. In his introduction to the third section of his book *Theories of Authorship*, John Caughie defines 'utterance' as an 'enunciating practice ... something in process at the moment of projection' (1981: 201). This defini-tion, as Caughie further explains, is ultimately related to Emile Benveniste's distinction between *histoire* (story) and *discours* (discourse) and consid-ers the statement only in its act of conveyance, thus raising the question of the enunciating subject who conveys. Caughie describes the distinction between a statement and an utterance as the difference between a 'product and a producing activity' (1981: 202). Livingston's use of the term is more indebted to Paul Grice (1969), who characterises an 'utterance' as an inten-tional (or purposeful), meaningful expression. By referring to an 'utterance' rather than a 'statement', Livingston indicates that authorship is not a lin-guistic practice that is then interpreted or modified for other arts and modes of expression. Instead linguistic authorship is only one form of authorship. This is a helpful strategy because it enables a general conception of author-ship that is not determined by conventional ideas and approaches to writing literature. Livingston's use of the term 'utterance' is not as precise as it could be, though. An 'utterance' is not an action, nor is it a reference to an action, except as a consequence of one. It is the *result* of expressing or communicating intentionally. Accordingly, Livingston's definition of an author can be revised as follows:

> Author* = the agent (or agents) who intentionally token(s) an utterance to communicate a meaning. 'To token' refers to any relevant action, an intended function of which is to compose an utterance; an utterance is the material form of an expression conveying a meaning within a symbolic system; and communicate implies the possibility of a receiver capable of understanding such an expression.[10]

The advantage of this redefinition is it focuses on the act of intentionally communicating through any symbolic system, such as natural language (spoken or written) or film.

The preceding analysis develops a generic, medium non-specific notion of authorship. The question is, does it accommodate film? One way to test this is to refine the general definition so that it becomes a medium specific model. The above definition of an author* can be adapted as follows:

> Filmic author = the agent (or agents) who intentionally token(s) a filmic utterance to communicate a meaning. 'To token' refers to any relevant action, an intended function of which is to compose a filmic utterance; a filmic utterance is the material film constituting an expression conveying a meaning; and communicate implies the possibility of an audience capable of understanding such an expression.[11]

None of the definitions above indicate the number of people that can author a work, only the conditions which must be satisfied to be counted as an author of a work. Crucially, 'meanings' are essential for a material form to be an 'utterance'. If a film lacks an utterance, it lacks an author. Test shots, wasted ends of reels and time-lapse films of flora used for scientific purposes do not, by themselves, communicate filmic utterances, so they lack authors. The time-lapse image may convey valuable information, but it does so as evidence rather than expression. If a film possesses an utterance, then the number of people who authored the film will be the same as the number of people who tokened the filmic utterance in that film. In most instances this will not be the same number of people that worked on the film, for the same reason that a novel written with the assistance of an amanuensis has only one author. Writing down words is different from composing a phrase. This obviously raises an important question: how can we identify whom, of all the people working on a film, contributed to its utterance. I will address this question presently.

By building theories of film authorship on theories of literature and literary authorship, film theorists and critics have questionably characterised film authorship as an act of individual expression, despite the collective nature of production. Obvious symptoms of this problem include Astruc's *caméra-stylo*, auteur criticism, various attempts to work out a semiotics of film, and author surrogate theories. Yet the literary model does not explain the *director's* privileged position. The director's prominence in film is a bit of an anomaly, especially when we consider that both theatre and television tend to privilege the writer. It is difficult to determine precisely why this is the case. One reason may be that early film prized spectacle over drama. Film was seen more as a branded entertainment. Filmmakers like Georges Méliès, Auguste and Louis Lumière, and Sagar Mitchell and James Kenyon, became well known by running and marketing their film companies under their own names. D. W. Griffith, as epitomised in his full-page advertisement, signalled the director's influence over the visual form and aesthetics as the essence of dramatic film art.[12] Writing in 1920, Eliot Stannard, an eminent silent film screenwriter, notes one reason why audiences recognised directors over writers:

> With the exception of sub-titles,[13] the Public *see* nothing of his [the Scenario-writer's] prose, it has already been of vital importance to both Producer[14] and actors, for it is through his style, erudition, and concise, unmistakable word painting that the Scenario-writer conveys to them his exact and perfectly visualised *dramatic* conception ...
>
> The public must realise that Producer and Scenario-writer are enormously dependent the one upon the other, since it is their *combined* work which is seen by the Public. And as a bad Scenario can hopelessly handicap a good Producer, so a bad Producer can irrevocably ruin a good Scenario. But if *both* be good, the Producer and the Scenario-writer working in complete harmony can then

achieve results which raise the Film industry from cheap-jack showmanship to the artistic level of Painting and Literature – of which, in a sense, the moving picture is the amalgamation, having the composition of the former and the psychology of the latter. (1920: 6–7; emphasis in original)

Without dialogue, silent films frequently masked the essential contributions of the screenwriter. Writing for film, television and theatre are not, in principle, remarkably different from one another, although clearly important formal and practical concerns distinguish them. Had film always been a recorded image *and sound* medium it is quite conceivable that the prioritisation of the director in the critical discourse could have been different. It is also worth keeping in mind that in the 1910s and 1920s European avant-garde artists gravitated to film and brought their artisanal practices with them. Even in the United States silent comedians like Roscoe 'Fatty'Arbuckle and Buster Keaton would start a film with little more than a guideline drafted and develop the film and sightgags as they went along. Whatever the reason, it seems that the equation of the director with the author of a work, while not entirely inaccurate, is more a product of historical contingency than analytical rigour. The definitions I offer above refocus attention away from production roles onto the intentional contribution to an utterance. Simply, to look to the director to find an auteur, based solely on a critical assessment of a film, is (1) too critically insensitive to the actual production history of any film to be useful; (2) to impose a literary model of authorship onto film; and (3) to conflate the critical concern of artistry with the more basic concern of film authorship.

David Bordwell and Kristin Thompson exemplify how this presumption of the director as author has become naturalised in Film Studies. They begin by separating authorship into a few different production categories. Solitary filmmaking, such as the films of Stan Brakhage and Carolee Schneemann, class the individual as the author. Films by collectives, such as the Kinoks, some of the NFB Studio B documentaries, and joint ventures like Hollis Frampton and Joyce Wieland's *A and B in Ontario* (1967–84), typically are classed as collective authorship because they involve a collaborative mode of production. So far so good. Bordwell and Thompson next assert that, for the most part, directors are the authors of the majority of commercial films because 'on the whole, the director usually has most *control* over how a movie looks and sounds' (2004: 40–1; emphasis added). To be fair to Bordwell and Thompson, developing a theory of authorship is not their key concern in *Film Art*. Their analysis, however, conforms to the traditional approach that has been applied to film authorship and auteurism. To begin with, they do not present evidence to demonstrate that the balance of control typically falls to the director. Even if it does, there seems no way to evaluate those instances where the director did not control the work. This would be essential for determining which films directors author. Bordwell and Thompson also do not make clear *how* one can determine what constitutes control in any production, or precisely what 'control over how a movie looks and sounds' really means, given the antecedent work of screenwriters, the financial pressures from producers and the personal touches added by cast and crew. Perfectly coherent products can be produced through the most chaotic procedures. Alternatively, films can be produced through highly devolved and distinct production roles, with directors having no, or at best limited involvement in scripting, casting, cinematography or editing, as happened often in the Hollywood studio period. In *The Genius of the System* (1988) Thomas Schatz challenges the director's centrality in Hollywood's studio era by demonstrating the substantial influence Hollywood producers and the studio system itself had on the film output during the period. Auteur critics, whether advocating the individual or the author surrogate, should recognise this, since they define auteurs as those directors able to make interesting and progressive films *in spite of* this dominating industrial structure. Bordwell and Thompson seem instead to defer to a critical tradition without substantiating its validity. It is ultimately a move that impedes, rather than promotes investigation into the genesis, both materially and semantically, of any given film. This tradition presumes directorial control and assigns authorship to a production role. The term 'author', though, is not synonymous with 'director'. A director's job is to control a production, while an author's job is to compose and convey meaning. Only if, in the process of controlling a film's production, a director also composes its expressions will that director be an author. This may be a frequent occurrence, but it is neither necessary, nor does it exclude others from contributing to the composition of a film's expression.

Although Livingston (1997) provides in his definition good cause and scope to test conventional approaches to film authorship, he privileges directors when elaborating his definition through hypothetical case studies.[15] His definition does not explicitly include the notion of control over the production of a film, yet he incorporates Bordwell and Thompson's assertion and builds it into his interpretation of a 'cinematic utterance'.[16] The term 'utterance' is absent in Bordwell and Thompson's overview. They focus on 'how a movie looks and sounds', not how it embodies an utterance. In order for Bordwell and Thompson's suggestion to be viable for Livingston, he needs to demonstrate that 'how a movie looks and sounds' and how it intentionally communicates or expresses an utterance in some way relate to one another. He does not do this, and as a result his conclusions, reasoned through these hypothetical case studies, drift away from his definition.

In his most recent book, *Cinema, Philosophy, Bergman: On Film as Philosophy* (2009), Livingston contests my assertion that the notion of 'control' is tacked onto his concept of authorship in his 1997 analysis.[17] He states: 'as long as authorship is deemed to be a matter of intentional activity (in the form of the intentional making of works), control, which is constituent of the latter, remains a basic component of this concept of authorship' (2009: 68). On this point Livingston and I seem to agree. I argued that making control a *separate* criterion was unnecessary, since it was already part of the definition of authorship through the notion of tokening an utterance. My disagreement was, and still is, with how Livingston applies the notion of control more broadly as a question of decision making and control over labour in film production, in addition to expressions of meaning. Livingston raises two examples to demonstrate his point. Re-examining them will help to explain the difference between our views. In the first, A and B work on a film for C, and C coerces them to produce the film 'along the lines indicated by C' (2009: 67). If this means A and B undertake technical roles to help produce C's film as C conceives it, then with Livingston I agree that neither A nor B has any claim to the authorship of the film. Depending on the precise activities A and B perform, this could be an instance of what Livingston calls 'individual authorship' or 'individual authorship in the context of a collective filmmaking process' (2009: 72–3). Livingston's other example is not as straightforward. A and B contribute to a film's artistic qualities, but A is in charge and B does what A asks of B. Livingston argues that this is not joint authorship, since A calls the shots. Livingston defines joint authorship as 'two or more persons work[ing] on an equal footing and shar[ing] responsibility for the final product' (2009: 73). Clearly A and B are not working on an equal footing

114

so this is not a case of joint authorship. However, between his two types of individual authorship and two types of joint authorship, there is space for a wider range of authorial practice.

The difference between Livingston's view and my own centres on our understandings of what is means to make or token an utterance. He proposes

> that the word 'authorship' is best used in the context of aesthetics and elsewhere to classify accomplishments that we evaluate as instances of expressive or artistic behaviour in various media, where authorship also involves exercising sufficient control over the making of the work as a whole. (2009: 71)

He distinguishes this notion of authorship from someone who authors a 'scientific paper or an instructional video'. Those creating these latter works are authors, but not artists (2009: 70). This is obviously correct. Authors of works of art and scientific articles are not fundamentally distinct, though. Both intentionally communicate meanings. The use of artistic conventions and objectives in the first instance and scientific conventions and objectives in the second makes the former an artistic author, the latter a scientific author. Calling these individuals an artist and a scientist respectively is a convenient linguistic simplification. In instances where these authors produce their works singly they are in control of both their expressions and works, not because there is requirement for a specific control criterion over the work, but because not to be in control would result in a failure to intentionally make or token an utterance. With single authorship there is no gap between intentionally making an utterance and being in control of the making of the work that conveys that utterance. Our disagreement centres on whether such a gap appears in collectively produced works. Livingston believes that it does appear and looks for the decision-maker to take responsibility for the single communication produced from the efforts of multiple contributors. My concern is this approach potentially masks the unique production histories of collectively produced works and does not necessarily retain the connection between the making of an utterance and the control of the final work.

Returning to Livingston's case of A and B's film may help to clarify the distance between our views. His example is fortunately quite vague, allowing for a wide range of interpretations of the relationship between these two individuals. Consider that A is in control of this film in the capacity of director. He is clear in his mind on how he is to control the production, and his cast and crew follow his instructions efficiently. Once his mind is made up he never wavers. However, A is inexperienced, though promising, and his knowledge of filmmaking and film construction is informed by a single textbook on classical film construction. B, an experienced cinematographer who has also worked as a director and editor, recognises A's limitations and inexperience. With the best intentions of aiding the director and helping to make a good film, B conceives of shots, lighting set-ups, microphone placements and blocking that all cohere to continuity rules and conventional scene development, and which also establish a highly intricate and sophisticated cinematic expression. A has a sense of the coherency and quality of the film emerging from this production, but is unaware that the look and sound has really been conceived by B, and B does nothing to alert A to this fact. B cannot overrule A, nor does he try, and A occasionally asserts his own view, providing at least some artistic input. Nevertheless, A usually accepts B's suggestions because they cohere with A's understanding of good filmmaking. A has control of the production and takes responsibility for it, but B has control of the utterance. Denying B a claim to a substantial proportion of the film's authorship seems wrong. Under Livingston's analysis, B has no claim to authorship because B was not in control of the production. All B could do was make suggestions. A recognised the consistency and coherency of B's suggestions, made sound artistic decisions by accepting them, and took responsibility for the finished work. Nevertheless, he contributed about as much to the film's expression as a pianist does to the musical expression emanating from a player piano. Although the film that results gains the reputation of an artistic masterpiece, it seems, on Livingston's view, either A is unduly credited with 'individual authorship in the context of a collective filmmaking process' or the film lacks authorship because no individual or group both controls the production and intentionally constructs its expression.

Instead of extending the notion of control from the intentional utterance to the finished work, a better solution is to define collective authorship in such a way that no gap appears between the intentional utterance and the finished work. Such a model will still deliver Livingston's four categories of individual and joint authorship (see 2009: 72–3), but can also account for other cases where contributions to a film's meaning is distributed across a number of individuals and production roles. Livingston resists such approaches, maintaining the mere fact 'that other parties have, under the author's supervision, made artistic contributions to the work does not entail that these persons are also to be taken as expressing their own attitudes in the work' (2009: 73). The mistake here is the suggestion that all individuals contributing to the expression of a work must individually hold the attitude expressed. Supplementing the definitions of authorship above with a theory of collective intention and action can deliver a theory of collective authorship that produces collective expressions while not presuming that all members of the collective hold individually the views expressed by the collective. All that is required of the individual is the will and ability to act collectively.

Theories of collective authorship are not new. In *Multiple Authorship and the Myth of Solitary Genius*, Jack Stillinger has proposed probably the most rigorous analysis of collective authorship. Although his main interest is literature, he demonstrates that his argument accommodates plays and films also. He forwards three main theses. First, the practice of literary interpretation (and presumably the interpretation of any medium) is 'structured by biography' (1991: 9). One of the core justifications for this intentionalist and biographical view relates to the idiomatic usage of language. If biographical interpretations are outlawed, then so are understandings of idiomatic uses of terminology, phrases, thematic connections, metaphors and images, for instance, and how they can mean one thing in one work, and something else when used by a different author. To dismiss authorial conventions undermines the work as human expression, recasting it merely as a cultural artefact. Second, no work of literature is *ever* a solitary venture. Normal publishing practices involve interactions with editors who typically make alterations and corrections. Good practice refers these modifications to the author for approval, but these changes are nevertheless not the author's interventions. They are collaborations and should not be dismissed under the presumption of authorial control. Friends, family and colleagues also provide useful contributions. Stillinger's author is not a Romantic author, but an author fully embedded in and responding to social and cultural contexts. The named author is usually more of a *principal* author than a solitary one. Third, by looking at authorship through the lens of production history, Stillinger raises questions about the very notion of a completed text. Revisions of historical works of literature,[18] translations, restorations, and differences between drafts, manuscripts,

The robot factory in *THX1138: The George Lucas Director's Cut* (2004) – a digitally-enhanced shot not present in the 1971 version of the film

published versions and proofs, signal that texts have lives beyond their authors not because of the fluidity of language, but because people keep reworking many of them. If we were concerned with a single author's genius, then we should be interested in the first draft, not the version sifted through and altered by numerous people in the publishing process.

Film also demonstrates these types of external interventions. These can range from multi-language prints, directors' cuts, format changes, changes in ratios, and DVDs with their supplementary tracks.[19] Restoration of silent film in particular relies upon extensive research and choices to be made about such basic concerns as tinting and toning, varying print lengths and versions, musical accompaniment and frame rates. Then there is George Lucas who is reworking older material, such as *THX1138* (1971) and *Star Wars* (1977). Additionally, censorship laws result in prints differing from one country to the next. Are we to entirely dismiss all those multi-lingual films produced in the early sound period as abominations or ignore them as somehow inferior? These films may not have the 'purity' of the first language versions, but they are remarkably interesting artefacts in film history, and films that many people saw. If we have a plurality of prints, then we must certainly have an increase in the number of individuals with some form of authorial input into the released films. Giorgio Bertellini's discussion of *Metropolis* (1927) exemplifies the difficulty of the concept of an authoritative print:

> *Metropolis* was first released in Berlin, 10 January 1927. That 'first' version was already shorter than the one approved by the Censorship Committee on 13 November 1926, which was 4,189 metres long. In addition, as was a conventional habit for silent films, different 'national' versions were prepared for distribution. In particular, the 3,170 metre American edition, shorter by one fourth and with remarkable new re-editings and intertitles, soon influenced German domestic versions, which were then rearranged according to the American revision. (1995: 282)

This is, of course, before the ravages of history shorted the film further. The American print omits 'Scene n.103', 'Hel's Room', largely because of the 'unnecessary and misleading infernal connotation' (Bertellini 1995: 284). This cut, which changes the film's narrative, imposes an intervention on the film at the level of meaning. Bertellini rightly notes that the prelapsarian state of a film is a myth, and film restoration is ultimately an authorial practice. Similarly, Antje Ascheid (1997) argues that translating a film into a different language constitutes a new text because of the relationships between language, cultural and national identities. This is taken to extremes with *Il Gattopardo* (*The Leopard*, 1963). Geoffrey Nowell-Smith is highly critical of 20th Century-Fox's and Burt Lancaster's interference in the English- language version of the film, interference that was so substantial that Luchino Visconti claimed no responsibility for the print. For years this 'mangled and pathetic' version was the only one in circulation in the US and the UK (see Nowell-Smith 2003: 80). Clearly, not all acts of multiple authorship are collaborative. Despite the problems with the Lancaster/20th Century-Fox version, its existence is still an interesting fact in film history that has much to say about 'collaborations' between Hollywood and Europe in the 1960s. Variations between prints of any film require attention to changes in length, censored content and language, for instance, in order to better understand the reasons behind these differences. Research into these differences will often reveal attitudes to social, cultural and political concerns that would not be recognised with a presumption that any film has only one definitive form and one definitive author.

The main area of multiple authorship in film is, however, in production. Berys Gaut argues, as I have above, that our understandings of film authorship suffer from their foundations in models of literary authorship. Any single author theory, he maintains, simply does not account for the collaborative nature of production: 'Most films are highly collaborative, and collaborative in ways that affect their artistic properties: actors, screenwriters, producers, cinematographers, all leave their marks on the way a film looks and sounds' (1997a: 150). Obvious examples of this include Sven Nykvist's cinematography in Ingmar Bergman's and Woody Allen's films, or the change in tone in Allen's films when Mia Farrow replaced Diane Keaton (see Gaut 1997a: 164). Mervyn LeRoy was a highly competent director (as well as a producer), but his success owes a great deal to his collaborations. Films like *Little Caesar* (1931) and *Gold Diggers of 1933* are dominated by the

Little Caesar (1931): Edward G. Robinson plays Caesar
Enrico Bandello, aka Rico and Little Caesar

Gold Diggers of 1933 (1933): choreography by Busby
Berkeley

actor Edward G. Robinson and choreographer Busby Berkeley respectively, but to reassign individual authorship to the actor or choreographer is to misunderstand the manner in which these performances function within two films constructed to engage problems of the depression. A film like *The Unknown* (1927) owes a great deal to Tod Browning's sense of the macabre, but required an actor like Lon Chaney with the skill and physical dedication to interpret and perform the role of Alonzo the Armless. Gaut's proposal that 'rather than rigidly categorising films by their directors, films should be multiply classified: by actors, cameramen, editors, composers, and so on' (1997a: 165), seems one of the most obvious and sensible suggestions in the study of film authorship. 'The career paths of all cinematic artists need to be traced, showing how their work adapts to new contexts, demonstrating how each interaction alters the ingredients and flavours of the cinematic pot-pourri' (ibid.). Indeed, theoretical investigations into authorship have been somewhat unresponsive to work undertaken by film historians. This proposal marks a distinct and welcome shift in the conception of a film author, from presumptions based on a production role to analyses of meritorious contributions in a collective environment.

Although a biographical approach would seem to favour an intentionalist account, Gaut resists this option. He explains why through what he calls the 'minimal hermeneutic claim':

> The *minimal hermeneutic claim* holds that to interpret a film requires understanding what its maker(s) did ... Intentionalism does not follow from the minimal claim: there are many aspects of understanding what someone did that go beyond explaining it ...

such as characterising the action in various ways, and not all features of actions (or of films) need be intended. (1997a: 153; emphasis in original)

Gaut develops his solution to this problem along constructivist lines, arguing that constructed (or implied) authors will resolve the problem of accidental qualities of a film. If a spectator likes a film, because there is good cinematography, editing and directing, for instance, then this spectator will construct good ideal surrogates for these roles that can manifest the qualities of the film non-

The Unknown (1927): even when not performing as an armless knife-thrower, Alonzo (Lon Chaney) maintains his deception before Nanon (Joan Crawford)

accidentally. This seems an odd solution, since it shifts an understanding of what someone did to what we think they did. Granted, it solves the problem of knowing which aspects of a film are accidental and which are not, but only by creating other fictions in the guise of author surrogates. In chapters two and three I argued against such notions. They are nothing more than names for interpretations spectators already hold, and therefore seem to have little or no real function in interpretation. Without a presumption of intention, there is no objective or guideline to motivate and direct interpretation.[20] Inference in film spectation is not simply the process of making sense of the audio-visual material, but the obligation to understand why the film was constructed and presented as it was.

Any challenge to Gaut's anti-intentionalism does not dent the problem he poses to intentionalists: the more people involved in authoring a film, the more diluted intention becomes, since many intentions now compete through the work. To address the problem another tack must be taken. Although Gaut accepts collective action, he does not acknowledge collective intention. He seems to presume that collective action is coupled with multiple individual intentions. A theory of collective intention will resolve Gaut's concerns. The notion of collective intention may sound exotic, but it involves nothing other than normal social practices we undertake daily.

To explain this I will begin by elaborating the notion of singular intention. Most basically, to act purposefully entails an intent to do so. However, not all actions are intended. If I move my arm with the intention of answering the telephone, but in the process knock over my coffee, it does not follow that I intentionally knocked over my coffee, even though this was the result of my intentional action. Conversely, not all intentions are acted on. I may intend to go shopping, but not go because I cannot find my keys. Intentions also need not be readable from the intended action. This was demonstrated in chapter three through Deren's comments about spectators misunderstanding the end of *Meshes of the Afternoon*. Gaut sees such aspects of intention as a problem for a theory of authorship, but this is only because he requires a tight correlation between an intention, an intended action and an understanding of the action that reveals intention. This, however, underestimates criticism. Criticism is not necessarily the immediate apprehension of intention. It may involve research, close critical scrutiny, reason and debate to begin to sort through what was intended (meaning), accidental (significance, or possibly an error) and misunderstood.[21] We do this all the time in conversation. When we do not understand an interlocutor, we request that he or she elaborate so that we can understand what he or she means, and may even point out an unintended consequence of this meaning.

The problem for a theory of collective authorship based on collective action and intention is that there is no collective mind, or 'superagent', within which to locate collective intention.[22] This raises three questions. First, are there such things as collective intentions? Second, if the answer is yes, are collective intentions aggregates of individual intentions, or are they something else that cannot be reduced or analysed in terms of individual intentions? Third, what counts as membership of a collective? In his essay 'Collective Intentions and Actions' (1991) John Searle provides a coherent and serviceable account of collective intention. The human capacity for collective intention, for Searle, seems obviously true. All we need think of is something like a sports team executing a certain play or an orchestra performing a symphony. Without a notion of collective intention, he argues, there is no obvious explanation for coordinated action. With this in mind the next step is to determine whether collective intention is simply an aggregate of individual intentions, or if somehow collective intentions are more fundamental, but without recourse to the notion of a collective mind. Searle raises a number of problems for analysing collective intention in terms of individual intentions, but there is one that seems to me to be convincing and which addresses Gaut's suggestion about the dilution of intention in collective authorship:

> The notion of a we-intention, of collective intentionality, implies the notion of cooperation. But the mere presence of I-intentions to achieve a goal that happens to be believed to be the same goal as that of the other members of the group does not entail the presence of an intention to cooperate to achieve that goal. (Searle 1991: 406)

A 'we-intention' is a very basic capacity we possess as a social species. It enables us to act cooperatively to achieve objectives we cannot achieve singly. We can use the example of a symphony orchestra to illustrate this point. Is the performance of a symphony an aggregate of individual performances motivated by the belief that by performing one's part one is contributing to the performance of a piece, or is each individual performance motivated by the collective intention 'we will perform this symphony'? Although the first seems to account for what happens, and avoids any suggestions of a superagent, it lacks collective will. At best it relies on the individual intentions and actions of one person coinciding with the individual intentions and actions of the other people on the stage. The second option is the better option because it explains the cooperation between members. The playing of the instrument responds to the group intention to play the piece. It is the necessary action to achieve the we-intention. No individual intention is required.[23] This argument does not necessarily eliminate individual intentions, but where they appear they will be in parallel with collective intentions, not the cause of them. For instance, an actor wants to improve her career, so she wants to be in a film directed by a top director. When this opportunity comes along she takes it. She clearly wants the film to go well, so she adopts the collective intention to make the film and acts appropriately. In this case the single action, perform in the film, fulfils two intentions, an individual intention – to improve her career – and a collective intention – to make the film.

This leaves the third concern: who counts as members of a collective in film production? The answer to this question will allow us to address Gaut's charge that collective authorship weakens intention. The simple answer is: those that adopt and are able to realise the relevant collective intention. On a film set it is unlikely that the caterers will have an intentional attitude to the film itself. They are simply commissioned to perform a task. Next are those hired to work (or volunteer) making a film, such as the director of photography, grip, sound recordist, gaffer, actors, director, producer, screenwriter, editor, and so on. These are the types of roles that *typically* adopt the collective intention to make the film. At this point I am not considering authorship, only the intention to achieve, with other members of the collective, a completed film. It is important that we distinguish between authoring a work and manifesting the work materially. The processes of conceiving and communicating an utterance may be hopelessly inseparable in practice, but theoretically they are two distinct tasks. Taken as a whole, this collective's interest is not directed towards producing an utterance, so this collective is not authorial. By holding the intention to make the film, members of this collective perform their tasks to fulfil their obligation to the collective intention.

Within the production collective is an authorial collective. In certain films the authorial and production collectives will be identical. Many avant-garde films exemplify this. In commercial filmmaking the production collective will be much larger than the authorial collective. For a film to be collectively authored, there must be a filmic intention that the authorial collective utters collectively. Gaut's example of a profound disagreement between Spike Lee and Danny Aiello working on *Do the Right Thing* (1989) is a good example for explaining this. Lee, the film's writer, director, producer and star, thinks the character of Sal should be played as a racist. Aiello, the actor playing Sal, disagrees. Aiello wins the argument and Sal is portrayed as a rather complex character who, although well intentioned, retains a paternalistic attitude towards the inhabitants of Brooklyn's Bedford-Stuyvesant neighbourhood. The result is not Lee's preference, and possibly not entirely Aiello's. However, it is the approach agreed upon within the authorial collective. Dissention within the collective does not necessarily pose a challenge to collective intention because the idea of collective intention does away with the need for singular authority over intention. To hold a collective intention is already to accept that others can contribute to shaping and achieving the shared will.

This is true of the production collective, but more important for the authorial collective. Searle's notion of 'Background' provides a theoretical footing to understand this process:

Collective intentionality presupposes a Background sense of the other as a candidate for cooperative agency; that is, it presupposes a sense of the other as more than mere conscious agents, indeed as actual or potential members of a cooperative activity. (1991: 414)

A director typically (though not always) will help to shape the utterance, as will a screenwriter, and perhaps a cinematographer, an actor or even a sound recordist. Authorship is not determined by production roles, although some production roles are more conducive to being able to contribute to a film's utterance. A camera operator who simply lights, frames and shoots as told, and follows the industry's best practice without question or reflection on the specific film, will not have contributed to film's utterance, although her or his contribution may be central to representing the film's utterance well. A sound recordist who proposes a recording technique because she feels it will add to the film's meaning (and not just meet stylistic conventions or standard practices) will have participated in the cooperative activity of developing the film's meaning if other members of the authorial collective accept the sound recordist's suggestions. This is why Aiello and Lee's disagreement poses no problem for an intentionalist theory of collective authorship. By even engaging Aiello in a discussion of the role of Sal, Lee recognised Aiello as a member of the production team that also was able to contribute to the ideas the film communicates. Collective intention does not require the collective agreement of all the members of the collective, for the reason that these are individual ideas. One of the core principles of collective intentional action is collaborative agreement takes priority over individual preferences. If we look back at the orchestra we can clarify this. The tuba player feels that a piece of music will be improved if he plays bars 14–27 *fortissimo*, but the overall opinion of the conductor and the rest of the orchestra is that this section should be played *pianissimo*. If the tuba player ignores the will of the collective and blasts away, he has not acted to fulfil a collective intention, but an individual intention based on how he thinks the music should be played. If instead he plays the section *pianissimo*, even though he disagrees with this choice, the tuba player has undertaken an individual action to fulfil a collective intention. Similarly, that Lee eventually deferred to Aiello's conception of Sal simply means that the authorial collective accepted Aiello's conception of Sal as part of the utterance of the film, even though this may have differed from both Lee's initial and individual conception when he wrote the screenplay, and his personal opinion when directing the film. Lee is clearly the most important authorial contributor to *Do the Right Thing*, being the film's writer, director, producer and star, but by no means the only person involved in producing the film's utterance.

By focusing on the notion of the utterance derived from Livingston's definition it is possible to develop an analysis of collective authorship in film that does not escalate numbers to include any member of a production team. The consequence of this analysis is that the author(s) of a film cannot be identified simply by looking at a film's credits. Identifying who is and is not a member of the authorial team of any film is essentially an empirical and critical exercise relying on the best available evidence, rigorous interpretation of this evidence, and coherent reasoning and argumentation, and is always open to refinement and challenge. This does require a shift in thinking about collective authorship. In instances of collective authorship, intention is no longer located in any individual. It is instead in the collective will of the group – a will that may diverge from the individual opinions held by *any* of the members of the collective. Not all aspects of a film will be intended either. Hirsch's distinction between meaning and significance accounts for unintended aspects of a film. Shifting to a notion of collective intention does not require author surrogates because the spectator does not determine intention and meaning. The development of a collective intention in collective authorship is an actual process that can, in principle, be empirically researched. If we wish to develop a robust theory of film as both a communicative medium and a practical process, we must abandon mythical and romanticised views of authorship and get down to the hard graft of understanding, as best as evidence and reason allow, how and why films express what they do. Undoubtedly, however, distributors will persist in marketing films under the names of directors. Historians and critics of film will only perpetuate these myths if we continue to take them at their word.

6   CONCLUSION

Throughout this book I have been guided by two central tenets. First, conventional notions of the auteur mythologise filmmaking by attributing authorship solely to a director via critical preferences and presumptions about directorial control, rather than through any rigorous research into the actual conditions of film production. Second, people make films *for reasons*. Any attempt to understand film authorship must consider both authorial intention and production histories. Questions of authors and authorship are empirical questions of causes. Accordingly, I have developed my analysis of film authorship to account for the medium's mainly collaborative production practices and its capacity for communication.

Interest in the film author as the material and intellectual source of a film has been present throughout the history of the medium, and has always been contested territory. Many early film production companies and Hollywood studios endorsed a corporate concept of intellectual property ownership, classifying filmmakers as employees. Thomas Schatz's extensive study of producers and the studio system demonstrates how significantly the studios controlled and shaped their overall film outputs. This is not just a question of historical production facts, but the historical explanations we offer. The very effort to single out and study a filmmaker like Edwin S. Porter at the Edison Manufacturing Company risks providing the employee with an authorial status that had not yet been conceived in the industry. Charles Musser deftly avoids the trap of imposing mid-twentieth-century critical perspectives onto turn of the century filmmaking by contextualising Porter's role in the wider production and exhibition practices of the period. The idea that films were individual acts of expression had yet to be argued for, as Griffith eventually did in 1913 when he took out his full page advert in the *New York Dramatic Mirror*, and which was challenged a few years later by the Supreme Court. In contrast, the filmmakers and critics associated with the European avant-gardes of the 1910s and 1920s repeatedly proclaimed the artistic authority of the film artist. Following World War Two, French film critics rescued this notion of a filmmaker in the guise of the auteur, a view of filmmaking modelled on the notion of the solitary Romantic artist. These debates were rooted in film practice and mapped onto broader twentieth-century concerns about artisanal and industrial production.

With the institutionalisation of film studies in academia, debates about authorship shifted dramatically. The question 'who is an author of a film?' became in the 1970s 'are films authored?' The seeds of this shift are rooted in literary theory. The anti-intentionalism that took hold in the mid-twentieth century started as an argument about the conditions of validity in interpretation, but spilled over into the nature of authorship, questioning whether authors even had the capacity for intention independent of the ideas already embedded and circulating in language. Meaning rests with the reader, it was argued, but even this is ephemeral. Michel Foucault endorsed this project to some degree, but contended the *impression* of authorial communication was not vanquished from the reception of a text. He proposed an author function, a fictional surrogate of the author that named a 'discourse', but which did not make any claims about the intentions of the real writer.

Film critics and theorists of the period adopted this approach as a response to the overly romanticised and politically uncritical notion of the auteur. By divesting filmmakers of authority over the meanings of their creations, theorists valorised a symptomatic approach to interpreting films as a means for evaluating their underscoring ideologies. The search for great directors shifted from the recognition of artistic aptitude to 'excesses' in films that betrayed and undermined a film's determinant capitalist ideology. Not surprisingly, the most progressive films were often directed by the same directors that auteurist critics had celebrated previously. This theory, though, broke the connection back to the director. No longer was the auteur someone like John Ford, but 'John Ford', a critical construction emerging from the text. Despite intentions, this theory demonstrated critics' insatiable need to attribute the source of meaning to an individual, and was therefore a self-defeating approach. What possible interest could there be in a 'John Ford', a textual construction, unless it could somehow become reconnected to John Ford? Peter Wollen explains that it is the trace of the director's unconscious in the film that allows this connection back to the director. The theory failed to achieve this aim. This 'critic as analyst' approach, which Wollen later regretted, aimed to address authorship but ultimately had critics marvelling at their own theoretically determined interpretations. Ironically, Barthes' proclamation 'the birth of the reader must be at the cost of the death of the Author' always suggested this would be the case (1977a: 148). The abandonment of authorship as expression exacted a political price. Although developed with the best intentions of critiquing Western capitalism, these theories, in denying the author's conscious voice, also denied expression to underrepresented groups struggling to make their voices heard. This generated a rift within Marxist criticism. To challenge norms of gender, race and sexuality, the capacity for individual expression was necessary.

Empirical investigations into film authorship have become more prevalent since the 1980s, partially as a response to the improved situation for archival research. The appearance of extensive studies of directors, actors and studios, for instance, from across the history of film, as well as detailed studies of the production histories of individual films, have motivated re-evaluations of auteur criticism and the poststructuralist challenge to the author. This has been further reinforced by resurgent debates on intention through literary theory and speech act theory. The combination of this growing evidence of film productions and the influence of analytical philosophy on film theory has enabled a shift from a textual to a communicative model of film authorship. This shift allows us to refocus our attention from the coherent picture of a film's reception to the more complicated situation of its production. This I believe is an important development in our understanding of film authorship, not just because it promotes a historically robust understanding of the actual means by which any film comes about, but also because it provides a more accountable analysis of how films are meaningful and culturally significant. Historical research has demonstrated that films are collaborative enterprises and that authors are facts of film production. In my arguments characterising film authorship as collective intentional action I have simply aimed to refine ongoing debates in film authorship to forward a candidate theory that explains these facts.

NOTES

introduction
1. Film was not exhibited silently during the silent period. The arrival of sound cinema did not introduce sound to film, but fixed sound to film at the point of production.

chapter one
1. Peter Wollen has offered a spirited defence of Curtiz as an auteur. See Wollen (2003).
2. The advert is signed by Albert H. T. Banzhaf, Counsellor-at-Law, Personal Representative.
3. Abel notes earlier in his book that in the late 1910s and very early 1920s there were disagreements about whether it was the writer or director that was the author of a film. Louis Delluc's 1918 essay 'Notes to Myself: *La Dixième Symphonie*', anthologised in Abel's book, is interesting because in it Delluc argues that the film's success relates to the way in which the writer/director Abel Gance is manifest in the film, while its failings centre on 'the quotations of Heine, Charles Guérin, or Rostand which you [Gance] toss in our path' (1988a: 146). This is basically text-book auteurism that would be elaborated about thirty years later.
4. Christian Metz found his film language in the most common and conventional of classical film texts. He argues that film, because of its history of telling stories, has become a language. Film language is not comparable to natural languages, though. It lacks their basic structural units. Instead, he proposes, film language has developed as an extension of the poetics and rhetoric of literature. See Metz (1991), especially chapter three, 'The Cinema: Language or Language System?' (1991: 31–91).

5. Astruc assumes that any external interference in the filmmaking process will dilute or dismantle the coherency of the director's expression. This notion locates ideas in individual subjects rather than within an intersubjective framework. For a discussion of the problems of subject-centred versus communicative reason, see Habermas (1987).

6. In the early 1970s Graham Petrie offered a substantial critique of the 'directors only' approach to auteurship and argued that other contributors to a film's production must also be considered. See Petrie (2008).

7. Sarris first used the term 'auteur theory' in his 1962 essay 'Notes on the Auteur Theory', *Film Culture*, 21, (Winter 1962–63), which is reprinted in the various editions of Mast and Cohen's and Braudy and Cohen's *Film Theory and Criticism*. Sarris later revised this notion: 'At this late date I am prepared to concede that *auteurism* is and always has been more a tendency than a theory, more a mystique than a methodology, more an editorial policy than an aesthetic procedure' (1996: 278).

8. Sarris's definition of 'American' is not nationalistic, but aesthetic. He notes of his methodology that since 'the criteria of selection for this historical survey are aesthetic rather than social or industrial, "American" will embrace many undubbed English-language films produced abroad. As much as this encroachment on British and international cinema may smack of imperialistic presumption, the doctrine of directorial continuity within the cultural marketplace of the English language takes precedence here over ethnographic considerations' (1996: 16).

9. Some of the names he mentions include F. W. Murnau, G. W. Pabst, Sergei Eisenstein, Jean Vigo, Jean Cocteau, Marcel Carné, Roberto Rossellini, Luchino Visconti, Ingmar Bergman, Carl Theodor Dreyer, Akira Kurosawa, Yasujiro Ozu, Satyajit Ray, Roman Polanski and Andrzej Wajda. (Sarris 1996: 22–3).

10. Sarris singles out Lewis Jacobs, John Grierson, Seigfried Kracauer, Paul Rotha, Richard Griffith, Jay Leyda and Georges Sadoul (1996: 15).

11. I will discuss this notion of the 'distinguishable personality' in greater detail below in the context of Pauline Kael's criticism of Sarris.

12. I am not aware of the degree of Antonioni's technical competence. If Kael is incorrect in this instance, I suspect another director could easily be found who has directed important films but who lacks the technical skills Sarris demands.

13. I am referring particularly here to the chapter entitled 'Direction and Authorship'.
14. This reference to Nowell-Smith also appears in the first edition of *Signs and Meaning in the Cinema*, published in 1969.
15. Kitses reflects on the methodology and evolution of his study since it was first published in 1969 in his chapter 'Directing the Western: Practice and Theory' (2004: 1–25).
16. I will discuss such arguments in the next chapter.
17. See 'What is an Author?' in Foucault (1984: 101–20). The notion of the 'author function' will be discussed in the next chapter.
18. I will elaborate on this in the last chapter when considering the relationship between intention and action.
19. See Wollen (1972: 94–102) for his discussion of Ford's 'antinomies'.
20. In his 1998 edition of *Signs and Meaning*, Wollen intimates that despite reservations he had about Barthes' and Foucault's pronouncements about authorship, he still felt compelled to revise his 1969 edition to take into account contemporary poststructuralist perspectives. In 1998 Wollen does not wholly withdraw from this position, but maintains that biography and textuality should coexist in theories of authorship, rather than abandoning the former for the latter (1998: 179).
21. Both essays are reprinted in Nichols (1976). Nichols' brief introductions to these essays provide a succinct historical contextualisation.
22. This hardly does justice to the psychoanalytical acrobatics that Jean-Pierre Oudart provides throughout section 25 (525–29) of the dossier.
23. The editors remind us that Ford's characterisation of Lincoln is 'moderated by the fact that Ford is also, if not primarily, Irish and Catholic' (1976: 501).
24. The name of the director still floats uncomfortably through the essay on *Young Mr. Lincoln*, unable to claim authority for the film under consideration.
25. David N. Rodowick provides an excellent commentary on the development of Derridean poststructuralism and on ideological film criticism in chapters one and three of his book *The Crisis of Political Postmodernism: Criticism and Ideology in Contemporary Film Theory* (1994).

chapter two
1. There is little agreement about the periods of both New Criticism and Chicago School Criticism. Generally, both are mid-twentieth century

approaches to literary criticism, spanning from roughly the 1930s to the 1960s, although both still resonate with current approaches to criticism. For an introduction to New Criticism, see Eagleton (1983: 43–53). W. K. Wimsatt, a prominent New Critic, discusses Chicago critics in Wimsatt (1982: 41–65).

2. The core section of the latter piece, entitled 'The Exorbitant Question of Method', is reprinted in Burke (1995: 117–24).

3. The question of authorial intention, while a question of authorship, is also a question of interpretation. Steven Knapp and Walter Benn Michaels' reinvigorated the debate about intention in their 1982 essay 'Against Theory'. Knapp and Michaels contest the need for a theory of interpretation. They maintain that theories of interpretation fall into two categories: either 'methods designed to guarantee the objectivity and validity of interpretations', or theories that proclaim the futility of such an exercise. (1985: 11). The problem, they argue, is both sides of this polemic rest on a common mistake. Both separate what are inseparable: 'on the ontological side, meaning from intention, language from speech acts; on the epistemological side, knowledge from true belief' (1985: 29). Knapp and Michaels maintain instead that these are false distinctions, and that both terms in each pairing are synonymous. Although the consequence of their argument is generally in agreement with intentionalism, they reject this badge, since intentionalism is itself a theoretical view based on the separation of intention and meaning. If, as they state, meaning is 'just another name for expressed intention', then the categories of intentionalism and anti-intentionalism are meaningless. No theory of intention or reception is required. Knapp and Michaels see as absurd the notion that an author could intend something in writing a work, but that the work could mean something else. They agree that many things can be read into a work that may, for instance, identify clear symptomatic concerns in the production of the work. While a reader may be able to *find meaning* through such a critical activity, the reader has not considered the *meaning* of the text.

4. Training, educational and industrial films will typically be more like practical messages.

5. Although discussing single images rather than film, Flint Schier offers one of the clearest explanations of this that I am aware of. 'Grammatical rules tell us how to compose whole sentences from items of the

lexicon that have had their significance bestowed on them by convention ... Given the conventional interpretations of the lexical items in a sentence, and given the rules of grammar, the interpretation of the whole sentence is fixed'. The composition of a sentence determines its sense, so he concludes that sentences are compositionally strong. An image instead is understood by recognising first its significant parts without compositional rules required for sense. From this he concludes 'pictures are weakly compositional; sentences strongly so' (1986: 65–7).

6. Nietzsche's *The Joyful Wisdom* was published in 1882. The title was later retranslated as *The Gay Science*.

7. In Stephen Heath's translation of Barthes' essay the term 'author' with a lower-case 'a' refers roughly to Barthes' 'modern scriptor' and differs from the upper-case 'A' 'Author', or the Author-God. I will retain this convention for the remainder of my discussion of Barthes.

8. Whereas poststructuralists are interested in the instability of the sign, Foucault instead uses his 'author function' to establish discourse as an historiographic principle.

9. Not all discourses have authorial names like 'Marxism'. Expressionism refers to an approach to representing psychological states, and 'Frankfurt School' singles out a place where certain group of scholars worked.

10. Booth uses the term 'mock reader' in the 1961 edition of his text, but changes this to 'implied or postulated reader' in his 'Afterword to the Second Edition' after considering the wider understandings of this notion (1991: 422–3).

11. The theory of the subject is a complex area in film theory that shifted the focus of film from an object of study to a process of subject formation. The theory views individuals as subjects of a variety of social, political and cultural institutions that shape and reshape individuals. The abandonment of the director as author is premised on the notion that a director is a subject of language, institutions, ideology, cinematic conventions and so forth, and not wholly in control of them when directing a film. Similarly, spectators are also subject to these external determinants. It makes no sense to speak of an origin or meaning because these are under constant revision. Psychoanalysis, with its theory of subject formation, proved useful to theorists look-

ing to explain the instability of the subject embedded within politics, society and culture, while linguistics and Marxism were able to shed light on the nature of the institutions that shape subjects.

12. Chatman also accounts for the notion of an implied author across texts. He defines 'career-authors' as 'the subset of features shared by all the implied authors … of the narrative texts bearing the name of the same real author' (1990: 88). Throughout his work Chatman generally endorses Barthes' structuralist semiotics, especially that in *S/Z* (1974), but resists the extreme anti-intentionalism of Barthes' poststructuralism.

13. I will offer a challenge to this view in the final chapter.

14. This seems to me to be an illusion of intention rather than a real intention. An intention cannot be a consequence of an action, only the cause of one.

15. Wilson realises that some films have something akin to a real narrator, often represented through voiceover or clear demarcations that we are seeing a memory. His concern is a general narrative principle underscoring all narrative films rather than an occasional practice of some.

16. Currie also endorses this view. I will discuss this in the next chapter.

17. David Lewis, in his essay 'Truth in Fiction' (1983), argues that what is true of a fiction will be constrained by collective beliefs of the time of its creation.

chapter three

1. I use the term 'voice' to account for what could otherwise be described as a theoretically coherent channel of communication. The term 'voice' is a little unfortunate, since it suggests verbal communication in natural language. Despite this, it has the advantage of indicating synecdochically an agent, either actual or fictional, that expresses. I use the term to refer to any identifiable process of communication, which could be linguistic, gestural, tonal, and so on. The main voices are authorial and narrative, but I will also discuss briefly character and character narrator voices.

2. I will examine non-narrative film in the next chapter.

3. Jack Stillinger (1991) provides a very interesting challenge to this notion about literary authorship.

4. On occasion I use pronouns possessively, like 'Capra's films'. I intend this as a linguistically efficient means for referring to a body of work synecdochically through an identifiable and significant member of the

production team, in the same way one might refer to a sports team by reference to a significant player.

5. This is a complex debate about the metaphysics of fiction that would be a distraction to work through in detail here. I have argued this case elsewhere (see Sellors 2006). For the alternative view, I recommend starting with Gregory Currie (1990, 1995). My debate with Warren Buckland in the pages of *Screen* may also be illuminating (Buckland 1999, 2002; Sellors 2000b).

6. Colloquially when we state Watson and Holmes are friends we presume we are speaking of a world of fiction because these stories are so well known.

7. This notion of a dramatised narrator-agent is taken to extremes in *Lady in the Lake* (1947). Throughout the film the camera presents the optical point of view of the character Philip Marlowe, played by Robert Montgomery. We hear Montgomery's voice throughout the film, but only see him when Marlowe looks into the mirror.

8. In *Making Meaning* Bordwell reasserts his disagreement with a communication model of film narration, favouring instead what he calls 'a poetics of cinema' that focuses on the critic's detailed interpretative capacity. His poetics propose a mode of criticism that responds to the rich history of film practice and convention rather than one that squeezes all interpretation into established theoretical boxes. Although Bordwell prefers to abandon personification as an unnecessary complication for the practice of film interpretation, he nevertheless accepts its value in interpretation. Interpretative techniques like personification, he contends, 'accord with notions of comprehension that members of all critical schools share. Here I want only to suggest that we rely too much on this way of thinking and talking' (1989: 258).

9. This is not the only time this technique is used in the film. In the sequence of Hannibal crossing the Alps, a tree is centre-right in the frame allowing an exterior shot on the right of the frame to be matched with a studio set on the left.

10. I would like to thank Giorgio Bertellini for discussion on this point.

11. It seems that anyone that wishes to retain the notion of the implied author would have to accept that the spectator would have to take some responsibility for the racist meaning of the film, provided the spectator included racism in his or her reading of the film.

12. In *Mimesis as Make Believe*, Kendall Walton explicitly rejects the notion of film narrators that I will defend. Fictional truths, he contends, are for spectators to judge, not narrators to narrate. Films like *Hour of the Wolf* (1968) and *Rashomon* are exceptions, he explains, because 'how fictionally things are … depends (in part) on how fictionally they appear to Borg, or how fictionally they are described by the various witnesses' (1990: 358). *Pace* Walton, I see these as typical of narration, not exceptions. Any theory that accepts such character narrators but not controlling narrators proposes two different notions of narrators. By conceiving of a narrator as one that tells a story without requiring any presupposition that they composed the material text, I require only one notion of a narrator to account for character and controlling narrators.

13. It matters which comes first, story or film. Typically theorists examine film and derive a theory of narration from this. As a result, fiction has requirements in one medium lacking in others, like controlling narrators. This raises the problem that what it means for something to be fictional depends upon the medium under consideration. I invert this relationship. We must first understand what fiction is, then consider how fiction can be represented in any medium. This is not a question of mapping literary theory to film, but of understanding the basic aspects of fiction and the narration of fiction, which literary theory has elaborated on at length, and examining how these essential and contingent properties of fiction map onto film. This approach is not available for constructivists, since for them there is no fiction independent of reception.

14. One may also suggest that this is narrative information presented only to the audience. If so, one then needs to explain how the journalists came to know of Kane's last word, which returns us to explanation (1).

15. It is also interesting to note that between the scenes of Kane's death and Susan's failed interview is the newsreel sequence. News always came between Kane and his wives.

16. The shooting script also makes no mention of Raymond's presence in Kane's bedroom when he dies.

17. See also Clinton Heylin (2006).

18. 'Ideas' should be considered widely, including all aspects of form and aesthetics, as well as any consideration of the world within which we live.

19. Misreading is more complicated than this, but this thumbnail sketch will suffice for my purposes here.

20. The need for author surrogates is premised on subject-centred reason. This tends to bolster the Romantic appeal of authorship by separating, to a degree, an author from the world around them. In contrast, Jürgen Habermas proposes intersubjective reason, which locates reason not solely in the mind, but in the interactions between individuals in a social, communicative context – the lifeworld. See also Bertellini and Sellors (2002).
21. In the DVD commentary for *The Manchurian Candidate* Frankenheimer states: 'You know a lot of things have been said about this movie, but the thing that I really care about about [*sic*] this movie is that it was the first movie to take on Senator McCarthy.'
22. Discussions I had with an undergraduate student, Joanne Murray, about her dissertation on Frank Capra helped me to recognise the relationships between *The Manchurian Candidate* and some of the films Capra directed.
23. Sklar and Zagarrio note that scholarship on Capra and his films was, until the late 1980s, limited mainly to these films and Capra's autobiography *The Name above the Title* (1971). Since then restorations of Capra's films, especially those from his early career, have been made available, allowing for a more detailed historical picture of Capra's days in the Hollywood studio system. Sklar and Zagarrio's book *Frank Capra: Authorship and the Studio System* is an important contribution to this re-evaluation of Capra's career.
24. In *Mr. Smith Goes to Washington* this act is once removed, as Senator Paine, overcome with guilt for his role in silencing popular opinion, renounces Taylor, following Jefferson Smith's 'lost causes' speech.
25. In addition, the voiceover in *The Manchurian Candidate* cannot help but echo the voiceover in Capra's *Why We Fight* series (1943–45).
26. It is also worth noting the similar builds and facial features of James Stewart, Gary Cooper and Laurence Harvey.

chapter four
1. On this point I have benefited from discussions with Gracia Ramirez about her research into American experimental filmmaking.
2. Many of these techniques she adopts from Stan Brakhage.
3. My discussion of Brakhage is indebted to James (1989) and Sitney (2002).
4. This hardly constitutes a justification. My concern here is not to vilify

Griffith. His racial politics across his films are complex, and at times contradictory, although this does not indemnify him from his responsibility
for the film's racist premise, story and representational strategies.

5. For a start, the titles in the existing English-language print of the film
    are translated from Spanish, which were translated from English.

chapter five

1. Carringer offers a slightly different model of collaboration than I will
    defend here. His theory of collaborative authorship aims to determine
    the *principal*, but not sole author of a film. I develop what he would
    call a model of 'collective-authorship studies, which tend to regard the
    dispersal of agency as the given to be contemplated' (2001: 378). We
    differ in that Carringer proposes single principal authorship as part of
    his methodology, whereas I accept single principal authorship may be
    a conclusion drawn from an analysis of the evidence.

2. Steven Knapp and Walter Benn Michaels (1985) defend a similar position.
    Their argument with Hirsch is over the need for a *theory* of interpretation.

3. If one wishes to establish a theory of the auteur, all one needs to do is
    bolt onto a theory of authorship a compatible theory of art. If a person
    meets the criteria for being an author, and if the authored work meets
    the criteria of being art, then it would be reasonable to propose that
    this author is also an auteur.

4. The basic skeleton of the theoretical argument I present in this chapter
    I have developed more fully in 'Collective Authorship in Film' (2007).
    In this chapter I will focus more on its practical implications for film
    theory, history and criticism.

5. This is an area that needs further investigation. If I draw five straight
    lines on a page and state that they express my views about authorship
    I have not authored anything because there is no system or convention
    for a reader to interpret these lines. Determining which collection of
    moving images are capable of being read and which are not is a much
    trickier task.

6. How we understand stories and meanings from images is a complex
    area of inquiry that is outwith the remit of this book. What is important
    is that humans possess this capacity. This is not an innate capacity,
    but one that needs to be learned. A spectator with no knowledge of
    avant-garde filmmaking and no prompting on how to view these films

will likely not understand them. Genres, stars and stylistic trends in classical filmmaking are also conventions a spectator must develop some competency with to understand classical narrative films.

7. I would not want to foreclose the possibility that this piece of digital video could become significant as a found object, and as a result become an authored work in the way that *Fountain* (1917) is a work authored by Marcel Duchamp. The author of this work would be the person who repackaged the video as a meaningful expression, not the person who accidentally pressed the button, unless these both refer to the same person.

8. One may object that there is a textual meaning that can be read that is independent of any intention. A slightly odd example I used in my essay 'Collective Authorship in Film' will illustrate the problem with 'textual meaning'. A monkey types away randomly at a computer keyboard and is rewarded with a banana. While doing this, the monkey unintention-ally produces a collection of words indiscernible from *Henry V.* Highly improbably, but possible nevertheless. The monkey's version is not a play about a king, because the monkey has no concept of a play or a king. Nevertheless, the text is still readable. Now, consider that this act of typing is bound and placed on your bookshelf. You start reading this book unaware of its genesis. The moment you learn this is not written by Shakespeare, but by a monkey, you will likely reassess your interpretation. The book becomes a curiosity. The monkey's and Shakespeare's books mean different things because they were pro-duced with different intentions. All the monkey was trying to do was get a banana and had no intention to communicate anything about anyone named King Henry V. The only thing that book means is 'I want a banana'.

9. In 'Collective Authorship in Film' I distinguish between three levels of authorship: author as mere cause (author (M)), an intending author (author (IM)) and an artistic author or auteur (author (IMA)), where 'M' means something has been caused and can be read, 'I' means this something is produced intentionally, and 'A' that this intention-ally produced something is a work of art. I have tried to simplify my argument here. My objective in this chapter is to explain 'author (IM)', since this is the main category of authorship we encounter in literature and film. One may contend that we experience artistic authorship most

frequently. However, all artistic authorship (author (IMA)) is also intentional authorship (author (IM)), and not all works of literature and film are artistic. Therefore, author (IM) is the dominant category.

10. This definition is a revision of the definition I offered in 'Collective Authorship in Film'. It has the same meaning, but this version better defines its terms. Strictly speaking, my inclusion of 'meaning' in the definition of 'Author*' is redundant, as it is implicit in the term 'utterance'. I have retained this redundancy for clarity.

11. Livingston also modifies his generic definition to propose a film-specific account of authorship. His definition of a cinematic author echoes his general account. The definition of a filmic author I propose here differs slightly from both Livingston's definition of a cinematic author and my definition proposed in 'Collective Authorship in Film'. I do not view my redefinitions as critiques of Livingston's definitions, which I think are basically correct, only as clarifications.

12. The term 'director' is not entirely accurate for the earliest years of film-making.

13. Stannard is referring to what we now call 'intertitles'.

14. Stannard's use of the term 'Producer' refers to what we call the 'director'.

15. Livingston's case studies are in his essay 'Cinematic Authorship' (see 1997: 139–44). In 'Collective Authorship in Film' (2007) I contend that the conclusions he draws from his first two case studies, 'An Authorless Film' and 'Authorship without Authority', diverge from his definitions of authorship because he considers control over production rather than control over the composition and assertion of an utterance.

16. 'Cinematic utterance' is Livingston's term. I prefer 'filmic utterance' because it locates the medium of film whereas 'cinematic utterance' evokes the institution of cinema. I will use the term 'filmic utterance' throughout the remainder of this chapter.

17. Livingston's book was published too close to the completion of this book for me to examine his arguments as closely and thoroughly as I would have liked.

18. Shakespeare's works are obvious examples.

19. For more on this, see Deborah Parker and Mark Parker (2004).

20. For two defences of intentionalism, see E. D. Hirsch Jr (1985) and Noël Carroll (1992).

21. Stillinger (1991) illustrates his arguments with precisely this type of criticism.
22. 'Superagent' is Michael Bratman's term. See Bratman (1993).
23. Discussing individual intention, Searle provides another example that may help to clarify this point. You intend to shoot a pistol at a target. In order to achieve this action you do not first require an intention to pull the trigger. Simply pulling the trigger (A) fulfils the intentional action (i.a.) to shoot the gun (B). He notates this as 'i.a. B by means of A'. Collective intention follows the same structure 'i.a. collective B by means of singular A' (1991: 412).

FILMOGRAPHY

Directors' names have been left out of the Filmography intentionally. Conventionally, the purpose of providing directors' names in filmographic entries is to identify the films' authors, based on the assumption that directors are the authors of the films they direct. Throughout this book I challenge this assumption, and instead align authorship with the production of meaning rather than with a production role.

A and B in Ontario (1967–84, Canada)
All Quiet on the Western Front (1930, US)
Berg-Ejvind och Hans Hustru/The Outlaw and His Wife (1918, Sweden)
Big Parade, The (1925, US)
Birth of a Nation, The (1915, US)
Blowup (1966, Italy)
Cabiria (1914, Italy)
Cat's Cradle (1959, US)
Citizen Kane (1941, US)
Départ de Jérusalem en Chemin de Fer/Leaving Jerusalem by Railway (1896, France)
Dog Star Man (1961–64, US)
Double Indemnity (1944, US)
Dream of a Rarebit Fiend, The (1906, US)
From Show Girl to Burlesque Queen (1903, US)
Fuses (1964–68, US)
Georgetown Loop, The (1903, US)
Great Train Robbery, The (1903, US)
High Noon (1952, US)
Il Deserto Rosso/Red Desert (1964, Italy)
Il Gattopardo/The Leopard (1963, Italy)
Intolerance (1916, US)
It's a Wonderful Life (1946, US)
L'Avventura/The Adventure (1960, Italy)
Lady in the Lake (1947, US)
Le Bourreau Turc/The Terrible Turkish Executioner (1904, France)

Le Médecin du Château/The Physician of the Castle/The Narrow Escape
    (1908, France)
Le Mélomane/The Melomaniac (1903, France)
Lonely Villa, The (1909, US)
Loving (1957, US)
Manchurian Candidate, The (1962, US)
Mary Jane's Mishap (1903, UK)
Meet John Doe (1941, US)
Meshes of the Afternoon (1943, US)
Metropolis (1927, Germany)
Midnight Cowboy (1968, US)
Mothlight (1963, US)
Mr. Deeds Goes to Town (1936, US)
Mr. Smith Goes to Washington (1939, US)
My Ain Folk (1973, UK)
My Childhood (1972, UK)
My Way Home (1978, UK)
Pan-American Exposition by Night (1901, US)
Par le Trou de Serrure/Peeping Tom (1901, France)
Professione: Reporter/The Passenger (1975, Italy)
Queen Kelly (1929, US)
Rashomon (1950, Japan)
Reassemblage (1983, US)
Rocky (1976, US)
Scorpio Rising (1964, US)
Searchers, The (1956, US)
Skyscrapers of New York City (1903, US)
Star Wars (1977, US)
Sunset Blvd. (1950, US)
'Teddy' Bears, The (1907, US)
THX 1138 (1971, US)
Vargtimmen/Hour of the Wolf (1968, Sweden)
Why We Fight (1943–45, US)
Within Our Gates (1920, US)
Wo hu cang long/Crouching Tiger, Hidden Dragon (2000, China/Hong Kong/
    Taiwan/US)
Young Mr. Lincoln (1939, US)

BIBLIOGRAPHY

Abel, Richard (1988a) 'Photogénie and Company', in Richard Abel (ed.) French Film Theory and Criticism: A History/Anthology 1907–1939. Vol. 1 1907–1929. Princeton, NJ: Princeton University Press, 95–124.

_____ (1988b) 'Cinégraphie and the Search for Specificity', in Richard Abel (ed.) French Film Theory and Criticism: A History/Anthology 1907–1939. Vol. 1 1907–1929. Princeton, NJ: Princeton University Press, 195–223.

Allen, Richard and Murray Smith (eds) (1997) Film Theory and Philosophy. Oxford: Oxford University Press.

Allison, David B. (1973) 'Translator's Introduction', in Jacques Derrida Speech and Phenomena, and Other Essays on Husserl's Theory of Signs. Evanston: Northwestern University Press, xxxi–xlii.

Ascheid, Antje (1997) 'Speaking in Tongues: Voice Dubbing in the Cinema as Cultural Ventriloquism', Velvet Light Trap, 40, 32–41.

Astruc, Alexandre (1968 [1948]) 'The Birth of a New Avant-Garde: La Caméra-Stylo', in Peter Graham (ed.) The New Wave. New York: Doubleday, 17–23.

Audi, Robert (ed.) (1995) The Cambridge Dictionary of Philosophy. Cambridge: Cambridge University Press.

Bal, Mieke (1997) Narratology: Introduction to the Theory of Narrative. Second Edition. London: University of Toronto Press.

Barthes, Roland (1977a [1967]) 'The Death of the Author', in Image, Music, Text. Trans. Stephen Heath. New York: Noonday Press, 142–8.

_____ (1977b [1971]) 'From Work to Text', in *Image, Music, Text*. Trans. Stephen Heath. New York: Noonday Press, 155–64.

Bazin, André (1967 [1950–55]) 'The Evolution of the Language of Cinema', in *What is Cinema?*. Vol.1. Ed. and trans. Hugh Gray. London: University of California Press, 23–40.

_____ (1991 [1978]) *Orson Welles: A Critical View*. Trans. Jonathan Rosenbaum. Los Angeles: Acrobat Books.

Bennett, Andrew (2005) *The Author*. London: Routledge.

Bertellini, Giorgio (1995) 'Restoration, Genealogy and Palimpsests: On Some Historiographical Questions', *Film History*, 7, 3, 277–90.

Bertellini, Giorgio and C. Paul Sellors (2002) 'Breaking the Mimetic Contract: Notes on Ideology, Intersubjectivity and Film Theory', *Reconstruction*, 2, 1, On-line. Available at: http://reconstruction.eserver. org/021/Breaking.htm (accessed 20 July 2008).

Bogle, Donald (2001) *Toms, Coons, Mulattoes, Mammies, and Bucks: An Interpretive History of Blacks in American Films*. Fourth Edition. London: Continuum.

Booth, Wayne C. (1991 [1961]) *The Rhetoric of Fiction*. Second Edition. London: Penguin Books.

Bordwell, David (1985) *Narration in the Fiction Film*. Madison, Wisconsin: University of Wisconsin Press.

_____ (1989) *Making Meaning: Inference and Rhetoric in the Interpretation of Cinema*. London: Harvard University Press.

Bordwell, David and Kristin Thompson (2004) *Film Art: An Introduction*. Seventh Edition. London: McGraw-Hill.

Bordwell, David, Janet Staiger and Kristin Thompson (1985) *The Classical Hollywood Cinema: Film Style and Mode of Production to 1960*. New York: Columbia University Press.

Bowser, Eileen (1990) *The Transformation of Cinema 1907–1915*. London: University of California Press.

Bowser, Pearl, Jane Gaines and Charles Musser (eds) (2001) *Oscar Micheaux and His Circle: African-American Filmmaking and Race Cinema of the Silent Era*. Bloomington and Indianapolis: Indiana University Press.

Brakhage, Stan (2001 [1963])
'Metaphors on Vision', in
*Essential Brakhage: Selected
Writings on Filmmaking*. Ed.
Bruce R. McPherson. Kingston,
NY: Documentext, 12–13.

Bratman, Michael (1993) 'Shared
Intention', *Ethics*, 104, 97–113.

Brooks, Peter (1995) *The
Melodramatic Imagination:
Balzac, Henry James,
Melodrama and the Mode of
Excess*. New Edition. London:
Yale University Press.

Brownlow, Kevin (1983) *Napoleon:
Abel Gance's Classic Film*.
London: Jonathan Cape.

Brunette, Peter and David Wills
(1989) *Screen/Play: Derrida
and Film Theory*. Princeton, NJ:
Princeton University Press.

Buckland, Warren (1999) 'Between
Science Fact and Science
Fiction: Spielberg's Digital
Dinosaurs, Possible Worlds
and the New Aesthetic
Realism', *Screen*, 40, 2,
177–92.

____ (2002) 'A Reply to Sellors's
"Mindless" Approach to
Possible Worlds', *Screen*, 42,
2, 222–6.

Burke, Seán (1995a) 'The
Twentieth-century Controversy',
in Seán Burke (ed.) *Authorship:
From Plato to the Postmodern*.
Edinburgh: Edinburgh
University Press, 65–71.

____ (1995b) 'Feminism and the
Authorial Subject', in Seán
Burke (ed.) *Authorship: From
Plato to the Postmodern*.
Edinburgh: Edinburgh
University Press, 145–50.

____ (1998) *The Death and Return
of the Author: Criticism
and Subjectivity in Barthes,
Foucault and Derrida*. Second
Edition. Edinburgh: Edinburgh
University Press.

Buscombe, Edward (1981 [1973])
'Ideas of Authorship', in
John Caughie (ed.) *Theories
of Authorship*. London:
Routledge, 22–34.

Cahiers du cinéma, Editors (1976
[1970]) 'John Ford's *Young
Mr. Lincoln*', trans. Helen
Lackner and Diana Matias, in
Bill Nichols (ed.) *Movies and
Methods*. London: University of
California Press, 493–529.

Canudo, Ricciotto (1988 [1923])
'Reflections on the Seventh
Art', trans. Claudia Gorbman,
in Richard Abel (ed.) *French
Film Theory and Criticism: A
History/Anthology 1907–1939*.
Vol. 1 1907–1929. Princeton,
NJ: Princeton University Press,
291–303.

Cardwell, Sarah (2006) 'Patterns,
Layers and Values: Poliakoff's
The Lost Prince', *Journal of
British Cinema and Television*,
3, 1, 134–41.

Carringer, Robert L. (1996 [1985]) *The Making of Citizen Kane*. Revised and Updated Edition. London: University of California Press.

____ (2001) 'Collaboration and Concepts of Authorship', *PMLA*, 116, 2, 370–9.

Carroll, Noël (1988) *Mystifying Movies: Fads and Fallacies in Contemporary Film Theory*. New York: Columbia University Press.

____ (1992) 'Art, Intention and Conversation', in Gary Iseminger (ed.) *Intention and Interpretation*. Philadelphia: Temple University Press, 97–131.

Caughie, John (1981) 'Introduction to Part Three: Fiction of the Author/Author of the Fiction', in John Caughie (ed.) *Theories of Authorship*. London: Routledge, 199–207.

____ (1993 [1991]) 'Don't Mourn – Analyse: Reviewing the Trilogy', in Eddie Dick, Andrew Noble and Duncan Petrie (eds) *Bill Douglas: A Lanternist's Account*. London: British Film Institute, 197–204.

Chatman, Seymour (1978) *Story and Discourse: Narrative Structure in Fiction and Film*. London: Cornell University Press.

____ (1990) *Coming to Terms: The Rhetoric of Narrative in Fiction and Film*. London: Cornell University Press.

Ciment, Michel and Laurence Kardish (eds) (2003) *Positif 50 Years: Selections from the French Film Journal*. New York: Museum of Modern Art.

Comolli, Jean-Luc and Jean Narboni (1976 [1969]) 'Cinema/Ideology/Criticism', trans. Susan Bennett, in Bill Nichols (ed.) *Movies and Methods*. London: University of California Press, 22–30.

Cook, David A. (2004) *A Narrative History of Film*. Fourth Edition. London: W. W. Norton.

Cook, Pam (1981 [1977–78]) 'The Point of Self-Expression in Avant-Garde Film', in John Caughie (ed.) *Theories of Authorship*. London: Routledge, 271–81.

Currie, Gregory (1990) *The Nature of Fiction*. Cambridge: Cambridge University Press.

____ (1991) 'Photography, Painting and Perception', *Journal of Aesthetics and Art Criticism*, 49, 1, 23–9.

____ (1995) *Image and Mind: Film, Philosophy and Cognitive Science*. Cambridge: Cambridge University Press.

Delluc, Louis (1988a [1918])
'Notes to Myself: *La Dixième
Symphonie*', trans. Richard
Abel, in Richard Abel (ed.)
*French Film Theory and
Criticism: A History/Anthology
1907–1939*. Vol. 1 1907–1929.
Princeton, NJ: Princeton
University Press, 143–7.

_____ (1988b [1923]) 'Prologue',
trans. Richard Abel, in Richard
Abel (ed.) *French Film Theory
and Criticism: A History/
Anthology 1907–1939*. Vol.
1 1907–1929. Princeton, NJ:
Princeton University Press,
285–91.

Derrida, Jacques (1973 [1967]) 'The
Supplement of Origin', in *Speech
and Phenomena, and Other
Essays on Husserl's Theory of
Signs*. Trans. David B. Allison.
Evanston, Illinois: Northwestern
University Press, 88–104.

_____ (1976 [1967]) '...That
Dangerous Supplement...',
in *Of Grammatology*. Trans.
Gayatri Chakravorty Spivak.
London: Johns Hopkins
University Press, 141–64.

Dick, Eddie, Andrew Noble and
Duncan Petrie (eds) (1993)
*Bill Douglas: A Lanternist's
Account*. London: British Film
Institute.

Doyle, Sir Arthur Conan (1992) *The
Adventures of Sherlock Holmes*.

Ware, Hertfordshire, UK:
Wordsworth Editions.

_____ (1995 [1901–02]) 'The Hound
of the Baskervilles', in *The
Return of Sherlock Holmes*.
Ware, Hertfordshire, UK:
Wordsworth Editions, 15–119.

Dulac, Germaine (1978a [1928])
'From "Visual and Anti-
Visual Films"', trans. Robert
Lamberton, in P. Adams Sitney
(ed.) *The Avant-Garde Film: A
Reader of Theory and Criticism*.
New York: New York University
Press, 31–5.

_____ (1978b [1932]) 'The Essence
of the Cinema: The Visual Idea',
trans. Robert Lamberton, in P.
Adams Sitney (ed.) *The Avant-
Garde Film: A Reader of Theory
and Criticism*. New York: New
York University Press, 36–42.

Eagleton, Terry (1983) *Literary
Theory: An Introduction*.
Oxford: Blackwell.

Eckert, Charles W. (2008
[1973]) 'The English Cine-
Structuralists', in Barry Keith
Grant (ed.) *Auteurs and
Authorship: A Film Reader*.
Oxford: Blackwell Publishing,
101–9.

Epstein, Jean (1978 [1924]) 'For
a New Avant-Garde', trans.
Stuart Liebman, in P. Adams
Sitney (ed.) *The Avant-Garde: A
Reader of Theory and Criticism*.

New York: New York University Press, 26–30.

_____ (1981 [1926]) 'On Certain Characteristics of *Photogénie*', trans. Tom Milne, *Afterimage*, 10, 20–3.

Everson, William K. (1998 [1978]) *American Silent Film*. New York: Da Capo Press.

Faure, Elie (1988 [1922]) 'The Art of Cineamplastics', trans. Walter Pach, in Richard Abel (ed.) *French Film Theory and Criticism: A History/Anthology 1907–1939*. Vol. 1 1907–1929. Princeton, NJ: Princeton University Press, 258–68.

Foucault, Michel (1972 [1971]) *The Archaeology of Knowledge and the Discourse on Language*. Trans. A. M. Sheridan Smith. New York: Pantheon Books.

_____ (1984 [1969]) 'What is an Author?', trans. Josué V. Harari, in *The Foucault Reader*. Ed. Paul Rabinow. London: Penguin Books, 101–20.

Gaines, Jane (2001) '*Within Our Gates*: From Race Melodrama to Opportunity Narrative', in Pearl Bowser, Jane Gaines and Charles Musser (eds) *Oscar Micheaux and His Circle: African American Filmmaking and Race Cinema of the Silent Era*. Bloomington and Indianapolis: Indiana University Press, 67–80.

Gaut, Berys (1997a) 'Film Authorship and Collaboration', in Richard Allen and Murray Smith (eds) *Film Theory and Philosophy*. Oxford: Oxford University Press, 149–72.

_____ (1997b) 'Analytic Philosophy of Film: History, Issues, Prospects', *Philosophical Books*, 38, 3, 145–56.

Genette, Gérard (1980) *Narrative Discourse: An Essay in Method*. Trans. Jane E. Lewin. Ithaca, NY: Cornell University Press.

Gerstner, David A. and Janet Staiger (eds) (2003) *Authorship and Film*. London: Routledge.

Grant, Barry Keith (ed.) (2008) *Auteurs and Authorship: A Film Reader*. Oxford: Blackwell Publishing.

Grant, Catherine (2000) 'www.auteur.com?', *Screen*, 41, 1, 101–8.

Grice, Paul (1957) 'Meaning', *Philosophical Review*, 66, 377–88.

_____ (1969) 'Utterer's Meaning and Intentions', *Philosophical Review*, 78, 147–77.

Gunning, Tom (1983) 'An Unseen Energy Swallows Space: The Space in Early Film and its Relation to American Avant-Garde Film', in John Fell (ed.) *Film Before Griffith*. London: University of California Press, 355–66.

_____ (1990 [1986]) 'The Cinema of Attractions: Early Film, Its Spectator and the Avant-Garde', in Thomas Elsaesser (ed.) *Early Cinema: Space – Frame – Narrative*. London: British Film Institute, 56–62.

_____ (1991) *D. W. Griffith and the Origins of American Narrative Film: The Early Years at Biograph*. Urbana and Chicago: University of Illinois Press.

Habermas, Jürgen (1987) 'An Alternative Way out of the Philosophy of the Subject: Communicative versus Subject-Centred Reason', in *The Philosophical Discourse of Modernity: Twelve Lectures*. Trans. Frederick G. Lawrence. Cambridge, Mass: MIT Press, 294–326.

Hansen, Miriam (1991) *Babel and Babylon: Spectatorship in American Silent Film*. London: Harvard University Press.

Harcourt, Peter (1977) 'The Innocent Eye', in Seth Feldman and Joyce Nelson (eds) *Canadian Film Reader*. Toronto: Peter Martin Associates Limited, 67–77.

Hassan, Mamoun (2008) 'His Pain was Our Pain', *The Guardian*, 20 June. On-line. Available at: http://film.
guardian.co.uk/features/featurepages/0,,2286399,00.html (accessed 20 July 2008).

Heath, Stephen (1981 [1973]) 'Comment on "The Idea of Authorship"', in John Caughie (ed.) *Theories of Authorship*. London: Routledge, 214–20.

Henderson, Brian (1981 [1973]) 'Critique of Cine-Structuralism (part 1)', in John Caughie (ed.) *Theories of Authorship*. London: Routledge, 166–82.

Heylin, Clinton (2006) *Despite the System: Orson Welles versus The Hollywood Studios*. Edinburgh: Canongate Books.

Hillier, Jim (ed.) (1985) *Cahiers du cinéma, Volume 1, The 1950s: Neorealism, Hollywood, New Wave*. Cambridge, MA: Harvard University Press.

Hillier, Jim and Peter Wollen (eds) (1996) *Howard Hawks: American Artist*. London: British Film Institute.

Hirsch, Jr, E. D. (1967) *Validity in Interpretation*. London: Yale University Press.

_____ (1984) 'On Justifying Interpretive Norms', *Journal of Aesthetics and Art Criticism*, 43, 1, 89–91.

_____ (1985 [1983]) 'Against Theory?', in W. J. T. Mitchell (ed.) *Against Theory: Literary Studies and the*

New Pragmatism. London: University of Chicago Press, 48–52.

Holdsworth, Amy (2006) '"Slow Television" and Stephen Poliakoff's *Shooting the Past*', *Journal of British Cinema and Television*, 3, 1, 128–33.

Irwin, William (ed.) (2002) *The Death and Resurrection of the Author?* Westport, CT: Greenwood Press.

James, David E. (1989) *Allegories of Cinema: American Film in the Sixties*. Princeton: Princeton University Press.

Johnston, Claire (1988 [1975]) 'Dorothy Arzner: Critical Strategies', in Constance Penley (ed.) *Feminism and Film Theory*. London: British Film Institute, 36–45.

Kael, Pauline (1985 [1963]) 'Circles and Squares', in Gerald Mast and Marshall Cohen (eds) *Film Theory and Criticism: Introductory Readings*. Third Edition. Oxford: Oxford University Press, 541–52.

Kitses, Jim (2004 [1969]) *Horizons West: Directing the Western from John Ford to Clint Eastwood*. New Edition. London: British Film Institute.

Knapp, Steven and Walter Benn Michaels (1985 [1982]) 'Against Theory', in W. J. T. Mitchell (ed.) *Against Theory: Literary Studies and the New Pragmatism*. London: University of Chicago Press, 11–30.

Koszarski, Richard (1994) *An Evening's Entertainment: The Age of the Silent Feature Picture, 1915–1928*. London: University of California Press.

Lamarque, Peter (2002 [1990]) 'The Death of the Author: An Analytical Autopsy', in William Irwin (ed.) *The Death and Resurrection of the Author?* London: Greenwood Press, 79–91.

Lévi-Strauss, Claude (1981 [1958]) 'The Structural Study of Myth (extract)', trans. Claire Jacobson and Brooke Grundfest, in John Caughie (ed.) *Theories of Authorship*. London: Routledge, 131–5.

Lewis, David (1983) 'Truth in Fiction', in *Philosophical Papers*. Vol. 1. Oxford: Oxford University Press, 261–80.

Livingston, Paisley (1997) 'Cinematic Authorship', in Richard Allen and Murray Smith (eds) *Film Theory and Philosophy*. Oxford: Oxford University Press, 132–48.

____ (2009) *Cinema, Philosophy, Bergman: On Film as Philosophy*. Oxford: Oxford University Press.

Marcus, Greil (2002) *The Manchurian Candidate*. London: British Film Institute.

Marie, Michel (2003) *The French New Wave: An Artistic School*. Trans. Richard Neupert. Oxford: Blackwell.

Mast, Gerald and Marshall Cohen (eds) (1985) *Film Theory and Criticism: Introductory Readings*. Third Edition. Oxford: Oxford University Press.

May, Lary (1983) *Screening out the Past: The Birth of Mass Culture and the Motion Picture Industry*. London: University of Chicago Press.

Metz, Christian (1982 [1977]) *The Imaginary Signifier: Psychoanalysis and the Cinema*. Trans. Celia Britton, Annwyl Williams, Ben Brewster and Alfred Guzzetti. Bloomington: Indiana University Press.

_____ (1991 [1971]) *Film Language: A Semiotics of the Cinema*. Trans. Michael Taylor. Chicago: University of Chicago Press.

Mitchell, W. J. T. (ed.) (1985) *Against Theory: Literary Studies and the New Pragmatism*. London: University of Chicago Press.

Moussinac, Léon (1988 [1921]) 'Cinema: *Fièvre. L'Atlantide, El Dorado*', trans. Richard Abel, in Richard Abel (ed.) *French Film Theory and Criticism: A History/Anthology 1907–1939*. Vol. 1 1907–1929. Princeton, NJ: Princeton University Press, 249–55.

Musser, Charles (1991) *Before the Nickelodeon: Edwin S. Porter and the Edison Manufacturing Company*. Oxford: University of California Press.

Neale, Steve (2000) *Genre and Hollywood*. London: Routledge.

Nelson, Robin (2006) 'Locating Poliakoff: an Auteur in Contemporary TV Drama', *Journal of British Cinema and Television*, 3, 1, 122–7.

Nesbit, Molly (1995 [1987]) 'What Was an Author?', in Seán Burke (ed.) *Authorship: From Plato to Postmodernism*. Edinburgh: Edinburgh University Press, 247–62.

Nichols, Bill (ed.) (1976) *Movies and Methods*. London: University of California Press.

Noble, Andrew (1993) 'The Making of the Trilogy', in Eddie Dick, Andrew Noble and Duncan Petrie (eds) *Bill Douglas: A Lanternist's Account*. London: British Film Institute, 117–72.

Nowell-Smith, Geoffrey (1981 [1976]) 'Six Authors in Pursuit of *The Searchers* (extract)', in

John Caughie (ed.) *Theories of Authorship*. London: Routledge, 221–4.

____ (2003) *Luchino Visconti*. Third Edition. London: British Film Institute.

Parker, Deborah and Mark Parker (2004) 'Directors and DVD Commentary: The Specifics of Intention', *Journal of Aesthetics and Art Criticism*, 62, 1, 13–22.

Penley, Constance (1988) 'Introduction – The Lady Doesn't Vanish: Feminism and Film Theory', in Constance Penley (ed.) *Feminism and Film Theory*. London: British Film Institute, 1–24.

Perkins, V. F. (1972) *Film as Film: Understanding and Judging Movies*. London: Penguin Books.

Petrie, Graham (2008 [1973]) 'Alternatives to Auteurs', in Barry Keith Grant (ed.) *Auteurs and Authorship: A Film Reader*. Oxford: Blackwell Publishing, 110–18.

Rodowick, David N. (1994) *The Crisis of Political Modernism: Criticism and Ideology in Contemporary Film Theory*. London: University of California Press.

Sarris, Andrew (1985 [1962]) 'Notes on the Auteur Theory in 1962', in Gerald Mast and Marshall Cohen (eds) *Film Theory and Criticism: Introductory Readings*. Third Edition. Oxford: Oxford University Press, 527–40.

____ (1996 [1968]) *The American Cinema: Directors and Directions 1929–1968*. Cambridge, MA: Da Capo Press.

Schatz, Thomas (1981) *Hollywood Genres: Formulas, Filmmaking and the Studio System*. London: McGraw-Hill.

____ (1988) *The Genius of the System: Hollywood Filmmaking in the Studio Era*. New York: Pantheon Books.

Schier, Flint (1986) *Deeper Into Pictures: An Essay on Pictorial Representation*. Cambridge: Cambridge University Press.

Searle, John R. (1969) *Speech Acts: An Essay in the Philosophy of Language*. Cambridge: Cambridge University Press.

____ (1991) 'Collective Intentions and Actions', in Philip R. Cohen, Jerry Morgan and Martha E. Pollack (eds) *Intentions in Communications*. London: MIT Press, 401–15.

Sellors, C. Paul (2000a) 'In Defence of Fictional Narrators in Classical Narrative Cinema', in Graham Coulter-Smith (ed.) *The Visual-Narrative Matrix: Interdisciplinary Collisions and Collusions*. Southampton, UK: Southampton Institute, 61–6.

_____ (2000b) 'The Impossibility of Science Fiction: Against Buckland's Possible Worlds', *Screen*, 41, 2, 203–16.

_____ (2006) 'A Realist Account of Fiction', *Film and Philosophy*, 10, 51–66.

_____ (2007) 'Collective Authorship in Film', *Journal of Aesthetics and Art Criticism*, 65, 3, 263–71.

Shohat, Ella and Robert Stam (1994) *Unthinking Eurocentrism: Multiculturalism and the Media*. London: Routledge.

Singer, Ben (1995) 'Modernity, Hyperstimulus, and the Rise of Popular Sensationalism', in Leo Charney and Vanessa R. Schwartz (eds) *Cinema and the Invention of Modern Life*. London: University of California Press, 73–99.

Sitney, P. Adams (ed.) (1978) *The Avant-Garde Film: A Reader of Theory and Criticism*. New York: New York University Press.

_____ (2002) *Visionary Film: The American Avant-Garde, 1943–2000*. Third Edition. Oxford: Oxford University Press.

Sklar, Robert (1994) *Movie-Made America: A Cultural History of American Movies*. Revised and Updated Edition. New York: Vintage Books.

Sklar, Robert and Vito Zagarrio (1998) 'Introduction', in Robert Sklar and Vito Zagarrio (eds) *Frank Capra: Authorship and the Studio System*. Philadelphia: Temple University Press, 1–9.

Stam, Robert, Robert Burgoyne and Sandy Flitterman-Lewis (1992) *New Vocabularies in Film Semiotics: Structuralism, Post-structuralism and Beyond*. London: Routledge.

Stannard, Eliot (1920) 'Writing Screen Plays', in *Cinema: Practical Course in Cinema Acting, in Ten Complete Lessons. Lesson Six. London: The Standard Art Book*, 1–33.

Stillinger, Jack (1991) *Multiple Authorship and the Myth of Solitary Genius*. Oxford: Oxford University Press.

Thompson, Kristin and David Bordwell (2003) *Film History: An Introduction*. Second Edition. London: McGraw-Hill.

Truffaut, François (1976 [1954]) 'A Certain Tendency of the French Cinema', in Bill Nichols (ed.) *Movies and Methods*. London: University of California Press, 224–37.

Vertov, Dziga (1984) *Kino-Eye: The Writings of Dziga Vertov*. Ed. Annette Michelson. Trans. Kevin O'Brien. London: University of California Press.

Walton, Kendall (1976) 'Point of View in Narrative Depictive Representation', *Nous*, 10, 1, 49–61.

____ (1990) *Mimesis as Make-Believe*. London: Harvard University Press.

Wartenberg, Thomas E. and Angela Curran (eds) (2005) *The Philosophy of Film: Introductory Text and Readings*. Oxford: Blackwell.

Welles, Orson and Herman J. Mankiewicz (1971) *Citizen Kane: The Complete Screenplay*. London: Methuen.

Wexman, Virginia Wright (ed.) (2003) *Film and Authorship*. London: Rutgers University Press.

White, Hayden (1987) *The Content of the Form: Narrative Discourse and Historical Representation*. London: Johns Hopkins University Press.

Willemen, Paul (1981) 'On Reading Epstein on *Photogénie*', *Afterimage*, 10, 40–7.

Wilson, George (1986) *Narration in Light: Studies in Cinematic Point of View*. London: Johns Hopkins University Press.

Wimsatt, W. K. (1982 [1954]) *The Verbal Icon: Studies in the Meaning of Poetry*. Lexington: University Press of Kentucky.

Wimsatt, W. K. and Monroe C. Beardsley (1982 [1946]) 'The Intentional Fallacy', in W. K. Wimsatt *The Verbal Icon: Studies in the Meaning of Poetry*. Lexington: University Press of Kentucky, 3–18.

Wollen, Peter (1972) *Signs and Meaning in the Cinema*. Third Edition. London: Secker and Warburg.

____ (1996) 'Introduction', in Jim Hillier and Peter Wollen (eds) *Howard Hawks: American Artist*. London: British Film Institute, 1–12.

____ (1998) *Signs and Meaning in the Cinema*. Expanded Edition. London: British Film Institute.

____ (2003) 'The Auteur Theory: Michael Curtiz and *Casablanca*', in David A. Gerstner and Janet Staiger (eds) *Authorship and Film*. London: Routledge, 61–76.

INDEX